Charles Greely Loring

Reconstruction

Claims of the Inhabitants of the States Engaged in the Rebellion to...

Charles Greely Loring

Reconstruction
Claims of the Inhabitants of the States Engaged in the Rebellion to...

ISBN/EAN: 9783337133658

Printed in Europe, USA, Canada, Australia, Japan

Cover: Foto ©ninafisch / pixelio.de

More available books at **www.hansebooks.com**

RECONSTRUCTION.

CLAIMS OF THE INHABITANTS OF THE STATES ENGAGED
IN THE REBELLION TO RESTORATION OF POLITI-
CAL RIGHTS AND PRIVILEGES UNDER
THE CONSTITUTION.

By CHARLES G. LORING.

BOSTON:
LITTLE, BROWN, AND COMPANY.
1866.

RECONSTRUCTION.

CLAIMS OF THE INHABITANTS OF THE STATES ENGAGED
IN THE REBELLION TO RESTORATION OF POLITI-
CAL RIGHTS AND PRIVILEGES UNDER
THE CONSTITUTION.

By CHARLES G. LORING.

BOSTON:
LITTLE, BROWN, AND COMPANY.
1866.

CAMBRIDGE:

PRESS OF JOHN WILSON AND SON.

CONTENTS.

PART FIRST.

PART SECOND.

RECONSTRUCTION.

PART FIRST

CHAPTER I.

STATE RIGHTS—PRELIMINARY HISTORY OF.

THE question of the day with the people of the United States — and none of graver moment ever agitated the public mind — is that concerning the claims of the inhabitants of the several States, recently in open rebellion against the national Government, to be re-admitted to the exercise of the personal and corporate political powers and franchises which they enjoyed under the Constitution before they made war upon the Union in order to accomplish its destruction.

That, by reason of that rebellion and its suppression, those who were parties to it forfeited their rights, as individual citizens, to property, liberty, and life, of which they could at any time be deprived by due process of law, and to which they could be restored only by the pardon of the Government, no one who does not justify the rebellion denies. The only controversy is, whether citizens, thus under the ban of

the law, became, upon the laying-down of their arms
and profession of submission to the national Government, at once restored to their former rights, as
inhabitants of their respective States, to immediate
participation in the councils of the nation and to immediate agency in the administration of the national
Government.

The practical issue may be thus stated: whether
it is competent for the national Government, as now
administered, to impose upon the inhabitants of the
several States lately in open rebellion against it, such
terms and conditions of re-admission to the exercise
of their former political powers, in the administration of the national sovereignty, as it may judge
to be essential for its future security; or whether,
having laid down their arms and professed a readi-
ness to obey the laws, those inhabitants are entitled
to an immediate recognition of those powers as
matter of right, and to be permitted at once to re-
assume the exercise of them in the councils of the
nation.

In such a discussion, it is necessary that we have a
clear and definite understanding of the meaning of
the word "State," as used in the Constitution, and as
it should be used in any argument concerning it.
There is a great deal of vague impression and loose
talk about the States of the Union as being sovereign, free, and independent; affording shelter for
much sophistry and declamation, tending to obscure a

subject which, above all others of the day, demands careful analysis and calm reasoning.

The simple definition of a State, politically speaking, is a people inhabiting a definite territory, and possessing an organized government to which they owe obedience ; and this definition applies exactly to the several States of the ¡Union. But there are various kinds of such States.

Some are possessed of absolute sovereignty, both internal and external, having not only entire control over the municipal relations and affairs of their subjects, but also unlimited power over their external relations to other nations. These constitute and are universally recognized as individual nations, or members of the family of nations.

There are others, which, existing as independent communities and possessing supreme authority internally over their subjects, have nevertheless no separate national sovereignty, but are united with other States by a common league or compact, by which their external or national sovereignty is committed to a central authority, representing them unitedly as one nation ; they separately neither claiming, nor being recognized, to be distinct members of the family of nations.

Such States cannot be denominated sovereign, free, and independent States in any general or seemingly appropriate use of those terms, — not being so in the most important elements of State sovereignty, freedom, and independence; namely, those of national power and relationship to other nations.

In States of the first-named class, rebellion against the national sovereignty, in whatever form, is treason in every individual engaged in it, and punishable accordingly.

In those of the second, the rebellion of any one State against the central authority does not render any of its citizens guilty of treason against it, nor make him personally punishable for that crime or otherwise. It is simply the violation or breach of the compact by the State to which its subjects owe exclusive allegiance; and the only redress for the other parties is by war against the State, to compel the fulfilment of its obligations, or to obtain redress for the breach of them; and, if they succeed in the conflict, the State becomes a conquered territory, over which the victors have all the rights of war,—including, of course, those to prescribe conditions on which the subdued State shall be re-admitted to the league, or may thereafter exercise any internal or external sovereignty.

It was to this last-named class that the inhabitants of the rebel States claimed that they belonged; alleging that they were sovereign, free, and independent States, united by the Constitution as by a compact or league only, from which they had the right to secede, as States, at pleasure, or for justifiable cause, — they being the exclusive judges of the existence of any.

They claimed that they owed personal allegiance to their respective States, and not to the United States; and that, in the resistance by their States of the authority of the Government of the United States, they, as individuals, were not rebels or traitors, but persons acting in obedience to their allegiance to *those States ;* and *which, as such,* were alone liable, if the league or compact had been unjustly violated by such resistance. And this, it is generally understood, is to be one of the principal grounds of defence of Jefferson Davis, if not the only one upon the merits, should he ever be put upon trial for treason.

If this position be maintainable, it is d.fficult to perceive on what ground the rebel States can deny the authority of the Government, as the victor in the contest, to dictate the terms of peace, and the terms upon which those States shall be re-admitted to their former privileges, and to hold them in subjection as conquered States during its discretion.

Upon their own theory, therefore, and that still asserted by them as boldly as ever to be the only true one, there could be no question of the right of the Government to prescribe *any* terms of re-admission which it should think just and expedient.

But, in truth, the inhabitants of no one of these United States ever had political existence as a sovereign, free, and independent State, *possessing any external* or *international sovereignty ;* or *ever had any distinct separate nationality.*

The inhabitants of them were always, from the beginning, the people, or portions of the people, of one empire, which alone maintained and exercised international sovereignty, and upon whose protection and supreme authority, as such, they relied.

In short, the inhabitants of them have always been substantially, as under the Constitution they now are, *one people*.

Before the Revolution, and during its continuance up to the Declaration of Independence, they were inhabitants of colonies or provinces of Great Britain, claiming all their powers of internal government under her charters or commissions, and contending with her only for immunity from alleged violations of them. They made no claim to any sovereignty, internal or external, not directly granted by or derived from her, or belonging to them as her subjects.

They were in all respects integral portions of the British empire, and so portions only of one people. Every inhabitant of each colony had the entire and perfect rights of British citizenship in every other, and of carrying on trade and dwelling in it, under the laws and regulations of the empire, unobstructed and unrestricted by colonial legislation.

They carried on the war of the Revolution for some time under the title of the *United Colonies*, and for the declared purpose of a redress of grievances only, and with no avowed view of establishing any national independence.

The first Congress, which assembled in 1774, adopted the significant title, "The *delegates appointed by the good people* of these colonies;" thus emphatically declaring their union as one people, struggling in a common cause. They asserted, as great constitutional rights *common to all*, the liberties and immunities of the common law of England, and declared themselves as united for the *common defence* of those rights.

And thus was the incipient, and soon to become the irrevocable step taken to constitute themselves the citizens of a new empire or nation.

The delegates to the second Congress, in 1775, were principally chosen, not by the State legislatures, as representatives of the States, but by conventions of the people of the several colonies, as representing them; although, in some instances, they were chosen by the popular branch of the legislature, the choice being afterwards ratified by such conventions.

Soon after its assembling, and before its second session in September, actual war had commenced in Massachusetts, and was imminent in other colonies; and the Congress immediately proceeded " to put *the country* into a state of defence," as one common country. It assumed and exercised control over the military operations of all the colonies; created a *continental army;* appointed Washington commander-in-chief " *of the continental forces*," and, in a letter accompanying his commission, charged him to make

it his especial care " that the *liberties of America* receive no detriment." It also provided a continental
currency; directed reprisals upon the ships and mer-
chandise of Great Britain; established a treasury
department, general post-office; and regulated the
relations with the Indian tribes.

In short, the inhabitants of the colonies, before the
Declaration of Independence, had substantially established a national Government in the name and with
the general consent and approbation of the people,
and with all the principal attributes of a nation, excepting that of international sovereignty, which they
had not yet claimed. The struggle was as yet in
defence of their violated rights as citizens of Great
Britain, and carried on under the title of " The
United Colonies ; " thus still recognizing that relationship.

And it was not till after thus uniting themselves
as one people, engaged in a common cause, that they,
in conformity with the recommendation of the Congress, proceeded in their respective jurisdictions to
make provisions for local governments for the man-
agement of their domestic concerns, which their separation from the mother Government and the exigencies
of the times made necessary. So that the formation
of a national Government, revolutionary indeed and
with limited internal powers, but none the less national, acting as the agent, and in the name and with
the consent, of the inhabitants of the whole territory

embraced within the limits of the colonies, had been established by the union in one body of delegates representing them, and was in actual operation before the adoption of the local governments, called State governments, as they have since existed; and had itself recommended their formation as necessary means of accomplishing the purposes of its creation, — very significant facts, surely, in illustration of the true relations of the States to the General Government in their subsequent history.

By the Declaration of Independence in 1776, made "in the name and behalf *of the good people* of these colonies," it was enacted that they were " and of right ought to be free and independent States; that they are absolved from all allegiance to the British Crown, and that all political connection between them and the State of Great Britain is and ought to be dissolved;" and that their national title thereafter should be that of the " United States of America," — by which title they have ever since been universally recognized.

By these proceedings, the inhabitants of all the colonies, *acting as one people,* threw off their allegiance to the British Crown, and claimed to become an independent sovereign nation, entitled to all the rights and attributes of external and internal sovereignty in regard to all international relations.

They did not assert any pretension of becoming severally independent States, entitled to any such

2

sovereignty, in their relation to foreign nations.
They claimed no membership as individual States in
the family of nations; nor did they declare any independence of each other in any relations with them;
but asserted their right to be accounted and dealt with
as one sovereign people or nation, composed of the
inhabitants of all the States; and as such, and only as
such, have they ever since been recognized in all the
treaties and international relations of peace or war into
which they have since entered.

By reference to the Constitution of Massachusetts,
Part I. Art. IV. (which was adopted before the Articles of Confederation were executed), it will be seen,
that she, in asserting the right of her people to gov-
ern themselves as a free sovereign and independent
State, limits these rights to the exercise and enjoyment of every power, jurisdiction, and right "*which is
not, or may not hereafter be, by them expressly delegated to the United States of America in Congress assembled.*" Now, at that time the United States of
America was the *only nation* known or recognized, *or
claiming to exist,* as one of the family of nations, and
of which each State formed only a component part,
pursuant to the Declaration of Independence. No
disavowal of distinct or independent or sovereign
nationality could be more explicit.

The local allegiance, however, of the inhabitants
of each colony, before due to the Crown, was
declared to be transferred, not to the central national

Government thus established, but to the colony itself, or, in the language of a resolution adopted by the Congress, " to the laws of the colony." The relations of individuals to the national Government were nowhere defined, but left to construction upon the nature of this union of the colonies or States in a national sovereignty.

Hitherto there had been no written articles of confederation or agreement, by which the obligation of the States, or the authority of the Congress, or the nature of the central Government, were defined.

The powers of an external national sovereignty had been assumed and acted upon by the consent of the people ; but its internal authority, or means of maintaining itself, were all left to loose construction, or the voluntary agency of the several independent States to comply with their respective duties, resulting from the alliance.

Whether either of the colonies or States was so bound by this alliance as to be incapable of abandoning it at pleasure — being in the nature of a voluntary party to a copartnership without limitation of time, and without any right on the part of the other States to enforce its compliance with the requisitions of the Congress for the carrying-on of the war of independence, in which they had thus united — may perhaps be considered questionable ; although such abandonment would seem to be an obvious breach of good faith to the rest, with which it had embarked as in a common cause. But the decision of the question is immaterial, as it was soon finally disposed of before it was practically, if ever, raised by the subsequent Articles of Confederation.

The embarrassment and inefficiency evidently resulting from this state of affairs rendered some more definite bond of obligation and union essential; and the Congress in November, 1777, addressed a circular letter to the legislatures of the several States, recommending them "to invest the delegates of the States with competent powers ultimately, in the name and behalf of the State, to subscribe articles of confederation and *perpetual union* of the United States, and to attend Congress for that purpose on or before the tenth day of March next."

But it was not till 1781 that the articles were adopted, owing to many causes of delay, a principal one of which was the claims of several of the States to the Western lands, extending to the Pacific Ocean, which it was contended by the other States should be held in common, as purchased by the common blood and treasure of all of them; and which lands were finally ceded to the United States immediately after the articles were executed, thus constituting a most important further bond of national union, and an inestimable element of future wealth and power.

By these Articles of Confederation, the government was to consist of a single representative body called a "General Congress," in which were vested all the

powers, executive, legislative, and judicial, granted
to the United States. Each State was to maintain its
own delegates ; and, in the determination of questions,
the voting was to be by States, each State being
entitled to one vote. The agreement was styled
" Articles of Confederation and Perpetual Union "
between the thirteen States named; and this body
politic was styled " The United States of America."
Each State retained its sovereignty, freedom, and
independence, and every power, jurisdiction, and right
not expressly delegated to the Congress. And the
nature and objects of the Union were described as a
firm league of friendship between the States for their
common defence, the security of their liberties, and
their mutual and general welfare ; and the parties
bound themselves to assist each other against all force
offered to or attack made upon them, or any of them,
on account of religion, sovereignty, trade, or under
any other pretence whatever. The free citizens of
each State were entitled to all privileges and immunities of free citizens in the several States. All the
general powers of external national sovereignty were
vested in the Congress, — the powers of treaty, peace
and war, regulating the coin, creating public debt,
building and equipping a navy, determining the
number of land forces, and of making requisitions
upon each State for its quota of men and money.
The several States were prohibited from receiving or
sending embassies, or entering into any treaties with

foreign powers or with each other without consent of Congress.

In short, the Articles of Confederation constituted the people of the States, thus united, one nation, as entirely as it was practicable for any mere league or confederation of States to do so.

They were of essential importance in enabling the Congress to carry through the war. But after the peace, and when the bond of a common paramount interest and necessity had ceased, and State jealousies, rivalries, weaknesses, and selfishness had shown the entire insufficiency of such a compact for the necessary strength and respectability of the nation abroad, and its internal peace and security at home, the people became conscious of the necessity of establishing a closer bond of union as one people, under a common government, having internal as well as external sovereignty; to which each citizen should owe a personal allegiance, and from which he might claim protection; and whose powers for all national purposes should act upon each individual citizen directly, and not through the agency of State government.

And from this necessity resulted the Constitution, upon the nature and construction of which the solution of this question must now depend.

Such was the condition of the nation and of the several States at the time of the adoption of that Constitution, and such the evils which it was intended to remedy.

From this history, nothing can be clearer than the proposition that no one of these States had ever been free, sovereign, and independent in *its external*, however it may have been so in its internal relations; but with regard to them no controversy has ever arisen.

There has never been a moment, from the breaking-out of the Revolution, when the inhabitants of any one of these States ever pretended to be a separate people from those of any other State *in any national relation* whatever; on the contrary, they always claimed to be portions of the people of Great Britain at the outset, and to become exclusively one independent people after declaring their final separation from her. Rights of national citizenship were never claimed by the inhabitants of any particular State, as distinguished from those of any other State, but always as citizens of the United States, comprehending them altogether. It is true that they were internally divided into separate and distinct municipal governments, sovereign and independent in all that regards their domestic relations; and could contract as such States, as being entirely independent so far as they had not surrendered the power so to contract to the central Government.

But no one, it is believed, can contend, that, after the adoption of the Articles of Confederation, any one State could have broken off from the confederacy and made a separate treaty of peace with England, or allied itself to any other foreign power; or could have established any laws or regulations subversive of the common rights and interests of all, in their external relations with other nations or in those internal to each other.

To be sure, no such act would have constituted any personal crime on the part of any inhabitant of such State against the General Government, because they owed personal allegiance to the State only.

But the General Government would have had the clear and manifest right, in such case, to interfere, and by force of war, if necessary, to compel conformity by the State to the general compact, and to enforce its requisitions if disobeyed. Civil war was thus, indeed, the only remedy; and it was to provide against this evil and weakness, among others, that the Constitution was established. But, if the result of any such war had been the subjugation of the State, it is clear that it would have been at the mercy of the victor as to terms of future re-admission to the rights of the confederation.

At the time, then, of the formation of the Constitution, the inhabitants of the thirteen States, retaining the internal sovereignties of each of them, were united as one people or nation in all that regarded external sovereignty, or any claimed or acknowledged national existence; and were possessed of a vast extent of unoccupied territory as tenants in common and joint owners, which was to be divided into new States in union with them, and composing with them a common country, so fast as it should become peopled; and which was incapable of division or apportionment among them upon any principle on which it had been granted, — the only one recognized being that of a *national domain*.

They had become, therefore, essentially a nation under a government exercising unqualified external sovereignty, possessed of a common country, and needing only the surrender to it of a portion of certain independent rights hitherto preserved by them as separate States, which interfered with their enjoyment of the internal sovereignty essential for securing the blessing of a perfect nationality, and which the Constitution was destined to provide for.

CHAPTER II.

THE CONSTITUTION — FORMATION OF, AND INDIVIDUAL AND STATE RIGHTS AND DUTIES UNDER IT.

THERE was a provision in the Articles of Confederation for making alterations therein, by the assent of a Congress of the United States and of the legislatures of the several States. And in February, 1787, in the Congress then in session, a resolve was passed, reciting that whereas experience had evinced that defects existed in the present confederation, and a convention of delegates had been proposed to remedy them, "and such a convention appeared to be the most probable means of establishing in these States *a firm national government*," it was expedient to call a convention of delegates for the purpose of revising the articles, and reporting to Congress and the several legislatures "such alterations as should, under the Federal Constitution, be adequate to the exigencies of government and the protection of the Union."

The several States assented to the proposition, and appointed delegates to the Convention, which assembled at Philadelphia, in May, 1787.

Although the purpose of the Convention was to amend the Articles of Confederation, it was soon apparent from the common stock of information contributed by the delegates, of the utter inefficiency of any mere league or confederation to accomplish the ends desired, that nothing short of a consolidated national government, with full powers of maintaining itself internally, as well as externally, by direct action upon the individual citizens composing the nation, in regard to all that pertains to the exercise of national as distinguished from municipal authority, could answer to the national exigency.

And the final result of prolonged, laborious, and exhaustive discussion of the subject by the greatest men of that age, and who would have been not less distinguished in any other age or nation, was the present Constitution.

As, however, it far transcended any mere alteration or amendment of the Articles of Confederation, — being in fact the substitution of " a firm national government" over the whole people of the United States, in place of a league of the States, — it was clearly necessary to submit its adoption directly to the people, acting in their primary capacity, and not to the State legislatures, as mere amendments of the articles might have been and were intended to be; it being obvious that State legislatures could have no authority thus to transfer the personal allegiance of their citizens to that of a central government, or part with the sovereign power with which they were invested by the people under their several State constitutions.

The question was of the substitution of a *constitutional government* in the place of *a league*, and was
one, therefore, which the people alone, and not the
State legislatures, could lawfully decide.

The Constitution was therefore reported by the
Convention to the Congress for its approval and sanction, and by it the several State legislatures were
invited to recommend the assembling of conventions
of the people to decide upon its adoption or rejection ;
and it was finally adopted by the people, or their delegates to conventions called for the purpose of deciding
upon it, and thus became the supreme law of the
land. And by the nature and objects and letter and
spirit of this Constitution must the question at issue
now be decided, with the aid, where needed, of
such light as may be drawn from the previous history
above alluded to.

Now, up to the time of the adoption of the Constitution, the people of the several States had, as above
shown, become one people or nation, so far as their
external national sovereignty was concerned, the government of which resided in the general Congress ;
each of the States possessing the right of sending
delegates to that Congress, and the right to one vote
in its deliberations and decisions. But each remained
at the same time supreme and independent in its internal sovereignty, excepting in so far as the Articles
of Confederation imposed limits thereupon, — which
limits were few, but of essential importance in pro-

viding for the necessities of internal commerce and equality of rights between the respective inhabitants of the different States.

But by the Constitution all this was changed. By its express terms, the national Government was no longer to consist of a confederation of States, to be administered by their respective delegates, but a government of the whole people of the United States as one people, under one supreme sovereignty internally and externally so far as national sovereignty was concerned; a government of which the people were to elect the legislators and rulers by their own personal votes, as representing them, and accountable directly to them, and not as representing the States, or as accountable to them.

In short, it established a "firm national government" as supreme in all things, touching its external and internal sovereignty over its subjects or citizens, as that possessed by any other government of any other nation. The existence of the several States as independent and sovereign in their municipal or domestic relations, and as having certain rights and powers as constituents of the General Government, was, indeed, fully provided for, and an equal representation was reserved to them in the Senate, — a most wise and salutary measure for the preservation of that independence and sovereignty, and for constituting a most important check upon the popular body representing the whole people. It is worthy of remark, that, while in the Articles of Confederation the sovereignty, freedom, and independence of each State, and every power, jurisdiction, and right not expressly delegated to the United States in Congress assembled, are expressly reserved, not a word is found in the Constitution of *any sovereignty as derived from*, or *granted to*, or *existing* in *the States*. On the contrary, the declaration that " the powers not delegated to the United States by the Constitution, nor prohibited by it to the States, are reserved to the States respectively or to the people," conclusively shows that the whole people of the United States, as one people, were considered and intended to be recognized as the ultimate source of all national power and sovereignty.

The States were to enjoy all the powers they originally possessed not prohibited to them, and certain very important new powers granted to them, by the Constitution; the government of the United States was to possess all the powers thereby vested in it expressly or by necessary implication; and the inhabitants of all the States, *collectively as one people*, were made the depository of all other power whatsoever.

Much profitless discussion has taken place upon the manner in which the Constitution was adopted; the advocates of secession and other apologists of it asserting that the Constitution was the act, or creation of the State governments, in the exercise of State sovereignties, while others contend that it was the creation of the whole people of the several States, acting as one people, for the establishment of one national government.

Nothing is plainer, however, than that the *State governments* had nothing to do with the matter, further than to recommend to their several peoples to meet together and appoint delegates to conventions to represent and act for them upon the question of its adoption, and to report their decisions to the Congress.

This was the only course which was open to secure the uniform calling of such conventions, — to give the legislative sanction of each State to any transfer or surrender which the people might see fit to make to the General Government of any of the powers which they had heretofore vested in the State governments; and above all was the only mode of obtaining the true result of a popular vote of the whole people upon the subject; it being obvious that the various interests, opinions, and sentiments of the whole people could be far better ascertained by this mode of voting upon the question in divisions or districts, than it could be by a general vote, in which the majority of the whole might control and constrain the universal wish or interests of large and important sections of the country. It is undeniably true, that the people of each State were so far sovereign and independent that they could not be required to surrender that

sovereignty and independence, to the extent required
by the Constitution, without their consent; and this
would of necessity require the inhabitants of each
State to vote separately and collectively on the question.
But it is none the less true, that the decision was not by
the State governments in their corporate capacity, but
by the people in their primary capacity, deciding
whether they would or would not become one people
with those of all the other States, under one form of
entire national sovereignty.

But, be this as it may, the fact seems indisputable,
that the inhabitants of the several States, by the
adoption of the Constitution, did voluntarily unite
themselves as one people under one supreme national
Government invested with all necessary powers of
national sovereignty, internal and external, — a Government which claims from them, as individuals,
personal allegiance to its authority, and extends over
them personal protection; and which claims also from
the political bodies or States, of which they were also
members, allegiance as such States and compliance
with the corresponding obligations imposed upon
them, while extending also over them its protection
in the enjoyment of all their political rights as such
States.

The principal rights of individuals as citizens of
the United States, thus created by the Constitution,
were those of the elective franchise in forming the
House of Representatives; of protection in property,

liberty, and life under the laws; and the rights of universal citizenship in the territories and jurisdiction of each State. The principal rights of the States were the elective franchise of equal representation in the Senate; of protection in the maintenance of a republican form of government, and against foreign invasion and internal sedition; with the enjoyment, in common with the inhabitants of all the other States, of free and unrestricted trade and intercourse among themselves, and of equal commercial advantages in their trade and intercourse with foreign nations.

To which was added the participation in the sovereign power of enacting amendments to the Constitution, if Congress should elect that mode of submitting any to the tribunal of State determination.

All these powers, rights, and immunities were created by the Constitution, and made dependent upon its authority. They have no other origin, no other right to be; and necessarily involve, upon every principle of public or civil law, justice and good faith, corresponding obligations for obedience to its authority and fidelity to its support.

So far, therefore, is the proposition that the States created the Constitution, so often asserted, from being true, that the reverse is much more nearly so. It was the Constitution which conferred all the rights which the States derived under it, and now have, as

original grants. It was the people of the whole
United States which thus *created* and defined the individual, corporate, and political rights of all the parties
to it.

The only authors or framers of the Constitution
were the inhabitants of the several States in their
primary capacities, as the acknowledged fountains of
all political power, who thus changed the organi-
zations and political constitutions of the several States ;
taking from them certain hitherto existing independent corporate powers and immunities, and investing
them with certain new powers, immunities, and rights,
not before enjoyed ; imposing upon them certain new
duties and obligations, in order to adapt them to
the new order of things ; and uniting themselves as
one consolidated nation or people, in which all political power, not thus otherwise disposed of, was declared to be thereafter for ever deposited.

We have then next to ascertain what were the
relations of the inhabitants of the several States to
the national Government, and their rights and obligations as such inhabitants under the Constitution.

CHAPTER III.

STATES UNDER THE CONSTITUTION—RIGHTS OF REPRE-
SENTATION IN CONGRESS—CONDITIONS OF—EFFECTS
OF STATE REBELLION.

By the Constitution, entire nationality was substituted for confederation. While, as before stated, the
people of the several States retained their internal
sovereignty over their domestic relations, they surrendered to the nation all the attributes of external
and many of the most essential of those of internal
sovereignty; entered into obligations of allegiance
and obedience to the Constitution, and all laws made
in pursuance thereof, *as the supreme law* of the land;
and made an oath by persons elected to offices of
State to support the Constitution, essential to the
organization of their respective State governments.
In return for which, the Constitution conferred upon
the citizens of all the several States, or secured them
in the enjoyment of two distinct classes of political
rights and privileges, — one of these pertaining to
them individually as *citizens* of the nation; and the
other consisting of those which each has in combination with others as members of the political corporate
body or State of which they are inhabitants, including

those of representation in the Senate and House of Representatives in Congress.

The word " State," therefore, as used in the Constitution, can only be construed to signify one under a government organized according to its requisitions, recognizing its supreme authority, and admitting the duty of obedience to its provisions and to all laws enacted in conformity with it. If a State be not in this condition, although it may still exist as a State within the Union, its inhabitants remaining subject to the territorial jurisdiction of the General Government, and to the Constitution and the laws, and to compulsory obedience to them, — nevertheless, it is not a State contemplated by the Constitution as entitled to the rights of those who have remained in full communion under it. And this proposition, seemingly so self-evident, is made, if possible, more manifestly true upon examining its provisions touching the rights and obligations created by it. Take, for instance, the rights of representation in Congress, the immediate subjects of inquiry.

One of the most important of the rights or privileges which the Constitution confers upon every citizen of the United States as an individual, and that mainly involved in the consideration of the question in hand, is that of the elective franchise, in being represented in the House of Representatives in the national Government. This is obviously a national right, or one to which he is entitled as a citizen of the United States, to be exercised for the common welfare of them all. And the members of the House, elected by its exercise, are representatives of the nation, a portion of its Government, and, in no proper sense, representatives of the State, or in any way justifiable in regarding its peculiar interests otherwise than as component parts of the good of the whole.

But although the individual is invested with this franchise as a citizen of the United States, or as one member of the whole nation, and to be exercised for the common good, it is nevertheless one *granted to him as an inhabitant or member of the State to which he belongs*, and is inseparately connected with such membership; so that if the State should cease to exist as a duly organized State, within the provisions of the Constitution, or he should cease to be an inhabitant of any such State, the right or franchise would no longer exist, although he might continue to be a citizen, and, as such, answerable to the laws of the United States.

This is evident from the language and spirit of the Constitution. It provides that " the House of Representatives shall be composed of members *chosen* every second year *by the people* of the *several States;* and the electors shall have the qualifications requisite for electors of the most numerous branch of the State Legislature."

Again: " No person shall be a Representative who shall not, when elected, be an inhabitant of that State in which he shall be chosen." Again: "Representatives and direct taxes *shall be apportioned among the several States which may be included in this Union* according to their respective numbers." "The number of Representatives shall not exceed one for every thirty thousand, but each *State shall have at least one representative*." "When vacancies happen in the representation from any State, the executive authority thereof shall issue writs of election to fill such vacancies." The existence, therefore, of this franchise, although it is vested in the individual as a citizen of the United States, is nevertheless made dependent upon his membership of a State, regularly constituted within the Union, and upon the action of such State in prescribing his qualifications as an elector; and, in case of a vacancy, upon the will of the executive to cause it to be filled.

It follows, therefore, that, if the State, of which any citizen of the United States is an inhabitant, be not one duly organized, or otherwise be not in communion with the other States, in obedience to the Constitution and the laws, or shall have become by repudiation or any other cause not entitled to the rights and privileges of a State under the provisions of them, no inhabitant of such State can claim the right to exercise the franchise, however loyal he personally may be to the General Government, or however zealously he may have opposed such disorganization, repudiation, or rebellion, and so be an unwilling victim to its consequences.

It may seem a hardship upon the individual to be thus deprived of a right or privilege by the fault of others to which he is no voluntary party ; but it is an unavoidable consequence of his political condition as the citizen of a contumacious or rebellious State, rendering personal discrimination impossible.

This rule, founded in unavoidable necessity, applies, with the semblance of still greater hardship, to the property of innocent inhabitants of a State in rebellion against the national Government. If a State having jurisdiction of a definite territory, of which it is possessor, rebel against the sovereign national Government, and actual war has arisen between them, such territory is by public law considered to be enemies' territory, and all property within its limits, to whomsoever belonging, as enemies' property, giving strength and resources to the enemy, and, as such, liable to capture and condemnation ; so that, in the late rebellion, a vessel belonging to inhabitants of Richmond, and captured by a national vessel, was adjudged lawful prize, although the owners were citizens of the United States, and claimed that they had always been and were loyal to them, and in no sense voluntary parties to the rebellion. (Prize Cases, 2 Black's United-States Reports, 635.)

It may seem needless to discuss the point further, as the express language of the provisions of the Constitution seems to make it so clear. It may be added, however, that any other construction, considering

this right of suffrage to be wholly personal as that of
a citizen of the United States only, and not dependent
upon the relations of his State to the Union, would
involve, as a necessary consequence, the right of the
inhabitants of a State in actual rebellion to elect and
send representatives to Congress, so long as they remained without arrest or conviction for the crime of
treason by due course of law; for, until such arrest or
conviction, no civil right can be accounted lost or forfeited.

Such being believed to be the principles of construction applicable to the Constitution, we have next
to consider the effect of the rebellion upon the relations of the people of the State to the Union, in reference to their right of suffrage as citizens of the United
States, and to representation in the national Government.

Now, by the rebellion, which was in the name and
by the asserted powers and authority of the several
rebel States, assuming to act in their political capacities, it is manifest that all their respective constitutions or governments contemplated by the Constitution
of the United States, or in conformity therewith, were
entirely abolished; and that entirely new ones were
substituted, having no affinity with those remaining
as loyal States in the Union, and none of the elements
which were necessary to entitle their inhabitants
to participate in any rights of representation in the
national Government. The governments, which they

had before rebellion, were founded upon the unity of the people of all the States as one people or nation, owing personal allegiance, and upon well-defined and established constitutional relations to the central Government; and could not be lawfully organized without the taking of the oath of such allegiance by every legislative, judicial, and executive officer of the State. They were also possessed of certain limited powers, prescribed by the Constitution, and were under numerous specified obligations to the General Government; all which were *essential elements of their nature as States under the Constitution*, and on which the political rights of their inhabitants to be represented in the General Government were founded. But those governments, in all their essential relations to that of the United States under the Constitution, were utterly abrogated by the rebellion; and new ones were substituted, founded on the denial of any such national unity, or any such allegiance, relations, limits, or obligations. Nothing could be more entire than the total abolition of the old State governments as they existed at the formation of the Constitution, and continued up to the time of the rebellion.

When, therefore, the rebellion was subdued, it is manifest that there were no governments existing in the rebel States, in conformity with the Constitution, or which could entitle their inhabitants to the exercise of any political powers under it.

The people of these States were, as to the United

5

States, without any civil government which that of the United States was bound to respect, and subject entirely to its military authority, or to such governments as it should see fit to impose, until State governments, in conformity to the Constitution, should be again constructed.

All their inhabitants who had voluntarily taken part in the rebellion were criminals, who, as individual citizens, had forfeited their right to property, liberty, and life under the laws, for their attempt to destroy the Government of their country; and had in the same manner forfeited and lost their corporate rights of representation and participation in its Government. And as they could only be restored to the former, by authority of the Government, so it alone was to restore the latter. Those States, as to any organized constitutional government entitling them to representation in that of the United States, were utterly " without form, and void."

And such was then the universal belief and conviction of all the officers of the Government, and of the people of the loyal States, excepting those who had always sympathized in the rebellion, and who, at the least, are now entitled to the credit of consistency in taking the opposite ground.

No one was more emphatic in the assertion of this principle than the President, who, in an official proclamation, declared that those States " were deprived of all civil government;" and authorized the publication of his declaration in conversation that "the State institutions are prostrated, laid out on the ground, and *that they must be taken up and adapted to the progress of events.*"

So Mr. Seward, in his telegram of July 24, 1865, to the provisional Governor of Mississippi, said "the Government of the State will be provisional only *until the civil authorities shall be restored with the approval of Congress,*" And again, in that of Sept. 12, 1865, a little more than a year ago, to Governor Marvin, of Florida, he says, "It must, however, be distinctly understood, that the restoration to which your proclamation refers *will be subject to the decision of Congress.*" And the whole course of the President's conduct was in conformity with it. He held the inhabitants of those States, as he lawfully might and was bound to do, as under military control, and without authorized civil government; appointed provisional Governors; and interfered with, and *dictated terms for, the formation of their local governments.* All this was justifiable only upon the hypothesis that he was exercising his military authority, in order to bring the people into loyal relations to the national Government; but it was entirely inconsistent with the idea that the States had any lawfully established civil governments under the Constitution. For, if they had, he could with no more propriety have thus interfered with them than with those of Pennsylvania or New York.

And he continues to act on the principle that no such civil governments exist in those States down to this day. On what other principle does he justify interfering with the government of Lousiana, or calling the Governor, elected by her people, to account for his conduct, or passing judgment upon the lawfulness or unlawfulness of conventions assembled there, or on the actions of State officers? And by what right does he forbid and prevent the pirate Semmes from holding the judicial office to which he was duly appointed under the authority of the State Government of Alabama, if it has one which the Government of the United States is bound to respect? And by what authority did he order the soldiery of the United States to aid and assist the murderer Monroe, in putting down an assembly of loyal citizens of New Orleans, if the State of Louisiana is under a regularly constituted State government? Can he, or would he dare to, order the troops of the United States, to come to the help of the city police in any loyal State, unless on application by the State Government? Any right of such interference is prohibited by the Constitution. And, if the President were to be impeached for this interposition of military force in New Orleans, the only justification he could set up would be, that the State had no civil government, but one in subordination to his military authority as commander-in-chief, and that the interposition was necessary for the preservation of good order.

Considering, then, the proposition established, that the inhabitants of the disloyal States, by their rebellion and open war against the United States, had abandoned, lost, or forfeited all civil and political rights under the Constitution, including those of representation in Congress, the next inquiry is when and in what manner such rights might revert or be restored to them.

It is maintained by some that they were never lost, but continued in full force during the rebellion, — that is the doctrine of the minority of the " Committee on Reconstruction ; " but, if the above views be sound, it is obviously erroneous, and needs no further answer. Others hold that although these rights were suspended or in abeyance during the rebellion, and until peace was effectually secured by the exercise of military power, yet that, when that was attained, the inhabitants of those States were instantly re-instated in all their previous rights and privileges, and, upon re-organizing their State governments so as to bring them within the requisitions of the Constitution, they became entitled to representation and participation in the administration of the national Government. And this, perhaps, is the general belief of those who advocate the immediate recognition of those rights.

On the other hand, it is maintained that civil and political rights and privileges under the Constitution, being thus forfeited or lost by the voluntary flagrant treason of the inhabitants of those States, can only be restored by the permission and authority of that constitutional power against which they rebelled, and by which they have been subdued

It is much to be regretted, that this question has been too often, if not generally, discussed under a form which is believed to be, not only no true statement of the real issue, but one tending greatly to distort and obscure it; namely, whether such States, by reason of the rebellion of their inhabitants, were to be accounted as in or out of the Union. No such issue has arisen upon the facts, and the question in that form is worse than a merely profitless abstraction: it is a pernicious play upon words.

They, during and after the rebellion, were States in possession of defined territories, and under organized governments to which they professed allegiance. And they were clearly in the Union, in so far as their territories, people, and amenability to the Constitution and laws of the Union are concerned. The national Government still maintained its right of territorial jurisdiction over them, and of enforcing obedience to the Constitution and the laws, as fully as it ever had; and their inhabitants remained citizens of the Union, and entitled to all the civil and political rights and immunities which they ever possessed as such, excepting those which they had forfeited or lost or abandoned by their treason.

By that treason, each inhabitant has forfeited his liberty and life as the penalty of his crime, if the

Government shall see fit to exact it by due process of law; but, until arrest and sentence under such conviction, he is still entitled to protection and immunity, and the enjoyment of all the civil rights which he ever had resulting from such merely individual citizenship. And he may be restored to the future undisturbed enjoyment of them by an act of amnesty of the General Government, or by a pardon from the Executive after conviction and sentence.

But, with regard to the political rights of the inhabitants of a State in its corporate political capacity, — those of representation in the House and Senate, for instance, — these, as has above been shown, do not rest upon nor result from their individual citizenship, as citizens of the United States merely, but depend also upon the political relations which the State bears to the Union, and cease to exist whenever it has suspended, lost, forfeited, or abandoned the rights belonging to it as a State in its normal relations to the Government; and can be restored only by restoration of the State to those relations.

Such being, then, the condition of the States lately in rebellion, what are the rights and duties of the General Government in regard to them, and to the restoration of their relations, rights, and privileges as equal States in the Union?

CHAPTER IV.

POWERS AND DUTIES OF GENERAL GOVERNMENT IN RE-
LATION TO THE STATES IN REBELLION, AND WHEN
LEFT BY THE REBELLION WITHOUT ORGANIZED GOV-
ERNMENTS UNDER THE CONSTITUTION; AND TO RES-
TORATION OF THEIR POLITICAL PRIVILEGES UNDER
IT.—RIGHTS CONSEQUENT UPON WAR.

THERE is no express provision in the Constitution
relating to the rebellion of the inhabitants of a State
in its corporate capacity against the authority of the
United States, nor to any penal or other consequences resulting from such rebellion, excepting in
so far as any citizen of the State may be punishable
individually for voluntarily participating in it, as
above suggested. And hence it has been argued,
that, in such cases, the General Government has no
power to compel obedience or fulfilment of the obligations which the Constitution imposes upon the
several States.

This was the theory adopted by Mr. Buchanan in
the most perilous crisis of the country's history, and
from which the leaders of the rebellion derived their
chief encouragement to resist the national authority,
which, if duly exerted, might have saved her from
the terrible struggle that ensued.

And it is the argument still of secessionists and their sympathizers. A moment's consideration, however, seems sufficient to expose its fallacy. Upon looking into the Constitution, it is found to contain, among others, the following express provisions, applying exclusively to the States in their political corporate capacities as such, namely: " The United States shall guarantee to every State in this Union a republican form of government." " No State shall enter into any treaty or alliance or confederation," or " enter into any agreement or compact with another State or with any foreign power." " The citizens of each State shall be entitled to all the privileges and immunities of the several States." " *The Constitution* and *the laws* of the United States which shall be made in pursuance thereof, shall be the *supreme law* of the land." " The President shall take care that *the laws shall be faithfully executed.*" And " Congress shall have power for calling forth the militia to execute the laws of the Union, and suppress insurrection and repel invasion." And, in the face of these provisions, is it possible to believe that any one State may, at pleasure, impose a despotic or monarchical government upon an unwilling and oppressed portion of its people? or may enter into a treaty of alliance, offensive and defensive, with a foreign nation? or into one of commerce, with discriminating privileges in its favor, destructive of the interests of the other States? or may prohibit the citizens of the other States from enjoying the same privileges and immunities with its own within its borders, and expose them to loss of liberty and life upon undertaking to reside within them? or may openly violate the Constitution or the laws of the land, and set the Government of the United States at defiance? — and that there is no redress, but that these violations of the Constitution must be quietly acquiesced in as remediless? Are these provisions — so express, and so obviously essential to the internal peace, the prosperity, the unity, the sovereignty, and security of the nation, and without the power to compel the fulfilment of which it would cease to be a nation — meaningless words, a mere *brutum fulmen* " of sound and fury, signifying nothing "? Such a construction of the Constitution must be accounted palpable nonsense upon any other theory than that of the absolute right of secession. What, then, is the remedy, and what are the consequences involved in the application of it?

And it is obvious that war is the only remedy. Any effective denial or violations of these provisions of the Constitution by any State must be by forcible resistance of the lawful officers of the United States, civil or military, engaged in the duty of compelling compliance with them; for so long as they should continue to be practically obeyed, no mere protest against their obligation, by any mere manifesto or proclamation, would justify recourse to force of arms, any more than would the mere declaration of opposition to the Government, and of an intention to resist its laws by force of arms, amount to treason under the Constitution. And, if such forcible resistance be resorted to by a State, the case presented becomes at once that of an organized government, possessing territorial jurisdiction, and asserting sovereignty and independence internal and external, and, claiming the personal allegiance of its citizens as paramount to all other allegiance, taking up arms to repel the attempt of another sovereign State to enforce obedience to its asserted authority. And this is nothing less than actual war — civil war indeed, but none the less actual war — between sovereign States, or those claiming to be such, and attended with all the attributes and consequences of war according to the public law, or law of nations.

Now, one of the best-established principles of that code is, that, as there is no acknowledged arbiter or judge between the parties engaged in war, the victor has of necessity the right to dictate the terms of peace, provided that they be not inconsistent with humanity and the generally recognized principles of that code. And this rule, under certain limitations, is as applicable to a civil war as to one between sovereign States of no antecedent connections with each other.

Vattel thus lays down the law of nations on this subject: " A civil war breaks the bands of society and government, or at least suspends their force and effect; it produces in the nation two independent parties, who consider each other as enemies, *and acknowledge no common judge.* These two parties, therefore, must necessarily be considered as constituting, at least for a time, two separate bodies, two distinct societies. Having no common superior to judge between them, *they stand in precisely the same predicament as two nations who engage in a contest, and have recourse to arms.*"

Wheaton lays down the law to the same effect. (Dana's ed., § 296.)

And it has been expressly recognized and enforced by the Supreme Court of the United States in the Prize Cases, 2 Black's U.S. Rep., p. 638, in reference to the late rebellion.

War, therefore, being the only possible solution of a controversy between one of the States and the Government of the United States, involving absolute denial and violation of the duties and obligations of the State, — the only tribunal to which appeal for a final decision could be made, — neither necessity nor propriety required that it should be set forth in the Constitution, as the means of determining the issue made between them, any more than they would require the statement in a civil contract, that, if either should fail to fulfil the obligation which it imposed upon him, the other should have the right to appeal to a judicial tribunal for redress.

In this case, both parties did thus appeal to the only and ultimate tribunal between contending States, and took upon themselves respectively the consequences of its judgment.

If that judgment had been in favor of the confederate States, the sovereignty, independence, and right of secession which they asserted, would have been vindicated, and finally adjudged to them, as matter of future indisputable right. And the United States would not only have been bound by that decision, but might also have been justly, by the law of nations, compelled to enter into such stipulation, and give such security, as the confederate States might reasonably exact, to prevent the United States from ever thereafter re-asserting claims to their allegiance or obedience. But the judgment was against them, and a corresponding just right accrued to the United States, not only to enforce obedience to the duties imposed by the Constitution, and keep the confederate States under military control until the peaceful fulfilment of them could be relied upon; but also to require full indemnity for the wrongs and losses caused by the rebellion, including payment of the debt incurred in suppressing it, if the confederate States could re-imburse the amount of it, and any security which reason and justice might show to be necessary to prevent any future perpetration of the crime.

But the powers of the United States, as victors in such a contest, are by no means as unlimited as they

might be in a war with another nation of acknowledged independence. They cannot be considered as
extending to the absolute subjection and permanent
control of the confederate States as conquered territories, nor to the imposition of any such unqualified
terms, conditions, or exactions as the exercise of more
sovereign will and power might justify in such other
war.

The power to wage war upon a State in rebellion,
for the preservation of the Union, is a constitutional
power necessarily invested in the Government solely
for that purpose, and limited by that necessity. It
cannot, therefore, be exercised for any other end, nor
beyond the means justly and reasonably required for
its accomplishment. It cannot justify the holding of
the territories of the State as conquered or as provinces under military rule, or the depriving them of
the rights of civil government, or of their previous
constitutional privileges, any further than may be
necessary to enforce present obedience to the Constitution and the laws, and for security against danger
of future like disobedience or revolt. But so far as
the attainment of these ends may render the occupation and government of the State by military rule,
or the withholding of any civil rights and privileges,
essential, so far the right of such occupation, government, and authority is as obviously and indisputably
justifiable as was the right of waging the war to obtain those ends. And, as above stated, the Govern-

ment, as the victor, must, by the necessity of the case, be the sole judge of such necessity and of the proper security to be demanded; being governed in the exercise of its discretion by the limits of constitutional authority, as above stated.

This view, it is believed, furnishes a satisfactory answer to the insensate clamor raised against the advocates of the powers of the General Government as founded upon the rights of war, and by which demagogues and sympathizers in rebellion have attempted to darken the understanding of the people, and lead them to believe that the assertion of such powers is nothing short of advocacy of an usurpation, trampling the Constitution under the heel of military despotism, instead of being, as it truly is, a vindication of the only means which the Government possesses of self-preservation, and for maintaining the Constitution and the life of the nation secure against future like outrage and danger.

It surely cannot be pretended with any show of reason, that the States recently in rebellion could become entitled to immediate restoration of their former political powers and privileges, merely upon the laying-down of their arms and professions of submission to the Constitution and the laws, if it should be satisfactorily apparent that such surrender and professions were a mere subterfuge in order to obtain a suspension of hostilities with the intention of renewing them at a more favorable opportunity, or if they were made with the view of using those political powers and privileges as the means of accomplishing in another mode the same purposes for which they had been waging the war.

This would be to render the contest, and the victory purchased at such cost of life and treasure, barren and worthless indeed. Obvious justice and the humblest common sense alike dictate that the right to *secure* peace and future security, the only desired fruits of the conflict, is no less clear than the right to fight for them; and that, if it was humane and just for the nation to enter upon the war and sacrifice the lives of such hecatombs of the best and bravest of her sons and such incalculable treasure to protect the Constitution and the Union from violation and disruption, it can be no less humane and just to exact, as the condition of restoring her rebellious children to their former political powers and privileges under them, reasonable security against the repetition of the crime, whether in the field of battle or in the halls of legislation.

Nor in this connection is it to be forgotten, that the potitical powers and privileges to which immediate restoration is thus claimed are not any which the Government of the United States has voluntarily taken away from the rebel States, either as punishment for their offence or as indemnity for the future; but are those only which they themselves deliberately and wickedly cast away, repudiated and abandoned, in perpetration of the blackest and most fearful crime known in human society, — the blackest and most fearful, because involving, not only the breach of the most solemn obligations, but of necessity also the ruin of numberless happy families, the sacrifice of hosts of precious lives, the loss of countless treasures of national wealth and industry, — the crime of parricide against the most humane and parental government the world ever looked upon, against which they could not allege one instance of wrong or oppression ; the crime of fratricide, involving the shedding of torrents of brothers' blood, the making desolate of hundreds of domestic hearths, and the shrouding of thousands of homes in mourning to terminate only in the grave. Surely, it is not for those guilty of crimes like these, with hands stained with the blood of their victims, and their hearts and mouths full of bitterness and hatred of those who upheld the Constitution and the laws in this terrible strife, arrogantly to demand immediate restoration of the powers and privileges so impiously trampled under foot, that they may resume their former unhappily paramount influence and power in the councils of the nation whose life they have thus sought to destroy ; nor to resent as an insult the requisition of those whom they have thus cruelly and grievously wronged, that some security be given against the repetition of their crime.

Suppose, that, in the war of the revolution, England

7

had been successful and conquered the revolting colonies, and re-assumed her territorial powers and jurisdiction over them. What question could there be of her power to impose such terms as she should think proper, for restoration to them of their previous colonial rights under their charters, notwithstanding that, upon the laying-down of their arms, they were individually restored to the rights of citizenship until conviction of treason by process of law?

Or if a large portion of the inhabitants of any one State, composing entire counties or districts entitled to representation in the legislature, should rise in rebellion and expel the State government from these territories, carry on civil war, finally terminating in their subjection, what reasonable doubt could exist of the right to take possession of those territories, and hold them until peace and order should not only be presently restored, but also made reasonably permanent, by continuing the force necessary for that purpose so long as such necessity should continue, or until guaranties should be given such as to render it needless; the individual citizens meanwhile being left in the ordinary enjoyment of all their civil rights, excepting those only of representation in the State government? How can the war be said to be finally terminated until absolute security is obtained?

And upon what principle can like authority be denied to the Government of the United States over inhabitants of the States under its authority, until peace and the security for life, liberty, and property of all loyal citizens within their borders shall be secured, leaving to such inhabitants the enjoyment of all other civil rights but those which entitle them to take part in the Government?

The principle so confidently maintained, that the inhabitants of the rebel States, upon the laying-down of their arms, became at once restored to all their political rights as States, as well as their former civil ones as citizens, until convicted of treason, involves the palpable and enormous absurdity that they are thus restored, although such surrender was not only enforced upon them and was altogether involuntary, as is the truth here, but was with intent of resuming their hostile attitude again as soon as they could gather strength for the purpose, and although the danger of such resumption was palpably imminent, and although, in the mean time, they were perpetrating upon loyal citizens atrocious cruelties, from which the ordinary protection of civil law was entirely inadequate, and evinced a settled determination to continue such perpetration. The case need but be stated to make its absurdity self-evident.

Upon the principles of public law, therefore, applicable, to this extent, to civil as well as to foreign war, as founded in the absolute necessity of the case, the General Government has the sole power and the right to determine when the conflict has ceased, and upon what terms and conditions, consistent with the objects of the war, the inhabitants of the States in rebellion shall be restored to political equality as States in the Union.

CHAPTER V.

POLITICAL RIGHTS AND PRIVILEGES OF REBEL STATES
FORFEITED AND LOST.—RESTORATION MUST BE BY
ACT OF GOVERNMENT.—LAW OF SELF-PRESERVATION.

But independently of the right of the General Government to prescribe the conditions upon which the inhabitants of the rebel States may be restored to equal political privileges with the other States under the Constitution, as one resulting from the war, there are several other grounds upon which, as is believed, it may be satisfactorily vindicated.

As the Constitution contains no express provisions determining the status of the inhabitants of a State in rebellion, or their right to restoration of political privileges as a State under the Constitution, after subjugation or submission to the authority of the General Government, such restoration is necessarily one of construction, or implied right or power, to be settled upon general principles. And the proposition which first suggests itself is that the power of deciding upon the right of such restoration, and upon the terms of it, resides in the General Government *as matter of absolute and inevitable necessity.*

The Constitution is the supreme law, and the Gov-

ernment established by it was for the purpose of carrying that law into effect. The Government is the
sole agent of the people for this purpose, and so has
supreme authority to decide every question arising
under it, in the particular modes pointed out by the
Constitution where such questions admit of their
application, and by its own action where none such
are provided. The Government represents the whole
people of the United States in all matters of law
arising under the •Constitution, as in all other things
provided for by it; and has not only the power, but
is under the obligation, " to provide for the common
defence and general welfare of the United States,"
and " to make all laws which shall be necessary and
proper for carrying into execution the foregoing power,
and all other powers, vested by the Constitution in
the government of the United States."

The nature of the political relations of the several
States to the United States is obviously pure matter
of law. Any question concerning the violation or
forfeiture of them, or the right of restoration to them
if lost or forfeited, is also a pure question of law,
and one which must of necessity be decided. All
these and cognate questions are not outside of the
Constitution, but are questions under it, affecting its
existence and the existence of the Union, and must
be decided: the nation's life is at stake upon them.
If, then, no other tribunal has been appointed for
their decision, the General Government has supreme

authority to decide them: or, if they are of a nature
to be ultimately decided by the Supreme Court, still
the present decision, for the time being, until the
question can be brought before that tribunal, if it
ever could be, must be by the General Government;
for a present decision one way or the other by it must
be made. Inaction is as much a decision against the
right, as action is one in favor of it. It has therefore
the final, or, if not the final, the immediate right of
decision; and such decision is its present first duty
under the clauses above stated. No one will dispute
that the settlement of these questions is essential to
" the common defence and general welfare of the
United States." No one can question that Congress
is invested with full powers to " provide for that
defence and welfare." And no one can point out any
other tribunal by which the nature of them can be
adjudged, and the proper remedy applied.

The action of Congress, therefore, seems not only
justifiable, but an absolute necessity. All these questions being obviously matters of legal right, — of law
purely, — the decision and the provision for them
must of like necessity rest with the law-making
power, — that is, the Congress, — or with the judiciary
And nothing can seem more manifestly in contradic-
tion to all legal principle, or a plainer usurpation,
than for the executive department of the Government,
whose office is confined to the administration of the
law, to assume the right of deciding upon the nature

of those relations and the manner of their restoration.

The next proposition is, that State rights, being corporate rights or privileges or franchises only, belonging to the States as subjects of the national Government, and being lost or forfeited by their rebellion against it, never could revert or be recovered by their subjugation or submission; but any restoration of them must be, by a grant from the sovereign power which created them.

State rights and powers are such, and such only, as were granted, defined, or recognized by the Constitution. The States are in no sense sovereign under it, nor are they in any part of it styled or recognized to be such. *They have no right to decide any question under it in the last resort*, but are always amenable and subject to the final decision of the General Goverment upon it. In certain cases they may sue and be sued, and in such cases must submit to the judgment of the supreme judicial authority, like any other subject. They are component parts of the nation as " bodies politic," or " corporate bodies," or " political societies" as Mr. Madison styles them, in the same manner as individual citizens are component parts of it. However distasteful the truth may be to the magniloquent advocates of State rights, the truth, nevertheless, is, that the *States are subjects* of the Government established by the Constitution, and bound by the law in the same manner as other subjects.

The right of representation in Congress, and so to participate in the administration of the General Government, was not one belonging to them in their original capacities when the Constitution was formed, nor one created by them as the framers of the Constitution. It was one conferred upon and granted to them by the whole people of the United States, in the formation of that frame or structure of government. *The people of the United States was the grantor, and the several States respectively were the grantees, of that right.* It was not one which they had the power to lay down and re-assume at pleasure. Such a principle would be obviously destructive of a government created for the ruling and preservation of a nation; but the right was given and made dependent upon the existence and fulfilment of certain relations and conditions prescribed by the Constitution, and in such manner that it could not exist unless they were complied with.

These rights, then, were merely corporate rights, belonging to the States only as political corporations or societies, and implying corresponding allegiance and obedience to the Government from which they were derived, in the same manner as do the rights and privileges of any other corporations created by a civil government. And it is not perceived why they may not be lost and forfeited by misuser or nonuser, in the same manner as may be any other corporate rights created by such governments. Nor is it seen

why Congress might not, in the exercise of its
supreme power of deciding or providing means for
deciding all questions of law arising under the Constitution, have provided a mode of trying and determining questions, like the present, concerning the
forfeiture or loss by States of their political rights
and franchises under it.

No such tribunal, indeed, could be necessary in an-
ticipation of flagrant rebellion and civil war, in which
such civil rights and privileges would be not only
renounced and abandoned, but the wealth and
strength derived from their enjoyment and the organization on which they were founded, were to be
the chief means of sustaining the contest against the
Government which created them. Such rebellion and
war, as has before been shown and seems to be self-
evident, is, of necessity, a destruction of any corporate
rights or franchise under the Government thus assailed
by the corporation itself. And, no other tribunal
having been established to pass in judgment upon
such forfeiture or destruction, the power of doing so,
if any judgment were needed, necessarily resides in
the Government itself in political as well as in legal
questions.

Another ground upon which these political rights
may be accounted as forfeited or lost is, that, as above
shown, they were granted upon condition of the continued existence of certain prescribed relations to the
United States and obedience to the Constitution and

the laws; and, that condition having been voluntarily and entirely broken, they were by the terms of the grant, and the principle universally recognized in continuing grants upon conditions, totally and irrevocably forfeited and lost. And, being so forfeited or lost, every principle and analogy of civil law and of common sense dictates that restoration of it must depend upon the assent of the other party; namely, the people who granted it, and who, for all purposes of upholding the Constitution and protecting the life and welfare of the nation under it, are represented by the General Government, which is invested with *plenary and final* power to determine all questions arising under it.

All analogy sustains this view of the subject. In all cases of contract, founded upon conditions, breach of the conditions is finally fatal to all rights under it, and their restoration could only be obtained by remission of the forfeiture by the other party. So, in cases of treason once committed, no penitence, no proffered return to allegiance, no obedience however entire, can wash away the crime: pardon from the government whose authority was violated can alone restore the guilty party to immunity in his former civil rights of property, liberty, and life. And it would be strange indeed, if criminals thus under the ban of the law, as having forfeited all their personal rights, including that of life itself, may still retain, in their political corporate capacity as a State, their

privileges and power of participation in the administration of the government which they sought and
may be still seeking to destroy, — strange indeed, that
the government should be invested with full power
to protect itself against danger from their treason as
individuals by the extremest punishment, but have
none whatever to protect itself against the infinitely
greater danger resulting from treason in their political corporate capacities as component parts of itself;
none to expel the most dangerous internal enemy,
but must continue to maintain and nourish the viper
gnawing at its heart.

It is no answer to pretend that the law against treason subjecting every individual guilty to loss of life is
a sufficient protection, as it may be administered to the
extent necessary for preventing repetition of the crime;
for, however sufficient that defence might be in ordinary cases of insurrection or conspiracy by compara-
tively few individuals acting in their individual
capacities, it is utterly and obviously incompetent and
futile in the case of a rebellion by the people, or a
large majority of the people, of a State, acting in its
corporate capacity.   Such punishment at the utmost
could be extended to a few only of those of most
prominent influence, position, or criminality. It could
never reach the mass of voters, who would be still left
to the uninterrupted and practically unassailable
enjoyment of their most important political rights, —
and those not only the most dangerous, but, it may be,

the only ones by the exercise of which they could peril the safety of the Government and the peace of the nation. Upon such a theory, the Government would be utterly powerless to protect itself from the hostility of traitors red-handed from the battles of rebellion, seeking to accomplish by political machinations the destruction they failed to accomplish on the field. It would seem that no merely technical construction of the Constitution, rendering the Government so feeble and incapable of self-protection, and for accomplishing the great ends of national unity, peace, and prosperity for which it was created, can be accepted; but that the common sense and the instinct of self-preservation alike cry out against it.

Again, if the theory referred to be sound; if the inhabitants of a State may thus rise in rebellion, and, after waging a bloody and costly war against the Government, may, by the mere laying-down of their arms and seemingly sincere professions of obedience, assert the absolute right of restoration to political station and power in the national administration,—it follows that the nation has no protection from revolt and national embarrassment or ruin beyond the mere pleasure of the inhabitants of any State, or number of States, to keep the peace; for if they may rebel, and, being conquered, may resume all their former rights,— or (to speak more properly according to the theory) if they have never lost any by rebellion,— it follows

that they may resort to this process, or the threat of it
(which in many cases would be hardly less disastrous
than the reality in a national point of view), whenever
they might think it expedient to do so, for the purpose of obtaining some desired political end or ascend-
ency, or of compelling the adoption of some especial
local or national policy, with the certainty, that, while
enjoying the chance of success, they could lose nothing
if defeated, and with the possibility that even defeat
might prove a gain, as in the present instance, where,
upon their theory, they would be entitled to re-assume
their former political rights, but with a vast increase
of relative power in the Government. And such rebellion might be endlessly repeated with the like impu-
nity, with the chances of gaining the desired end if
successful, and the certainty of sustaining no loss of
political power if defeated. The national Government, if of such a nature, would be little worth the
blood and treasure it originally costs for its establishment, or a tithe of those recently expended in its
preservation: it would be neither worth dying for
nor living under.

But there is another and broader view to be taken
of this subject, in the light of the great principles
upon which the Constitution was founded, and the
great purposes for which it was created, extending far
beyond any merely literal or technical rules of construction as applied to written contracts or instruments in
the ordinary business of life.

A constitution of national government demands more than mere obedience to rules of law founded upon *domestic* expediency, which renders their application to such instruments imperative and conclusive, often without much, if any, regard to the fundamental question of intention, or of right or wrong between the parties, or the purposes for which they were made ; and with none, if a technical rule can be found decisive of the question. Such rules are of inevitable necessity in the multifarious relations and commerce of individual life, and, in the long-run, subserve the cause of justice.

But a contract creating a nation, and designed to secure and perpetuate the internal and external peace and welfare, and to preserve the life of a nation, calls for very different rules of construction. The foundation principles of self-preservation and of essential security for the great objects of the compact, must have controlling influence over all other principles, if in conflict with them, when applied to any issue in which they are involved.

This principle of self preservation is fully recognized as one of established law in all civilized communities. A man, to save his own life, may destroy the life of another, although innocent of any wrong to him; as in the familiar illustration of two men upon a plank at sea sufficient for the safety of one, but not for both. Either may justifiably repel the other from it, if the instinct or duty of self-preservation be not over-

ruled by higher motives. And it applies with infinitely more force, and with no possible qualification,
where a national government is called upon to vindicate its existence, the destruction of which must involve
incalculable losses of life and of every thing that
makes life worth having.

Now, the Constitution of the United States was a
compact entered into by the inhabitants of the United
States for the declared purpose of erecting and maintaining " a firm national government," under which
they were to be united as one people, owing to it
individual allegiance as citizens of one nation, and
which was designed to possess all the powers of internal and external sovereignty requisite for securing to
them internal and external peace, security, and prosperity ; and any construction of it, therefore, which
renders it manifestly inoperative to accomplish these
fundamental objects, or incapable of resisting internal or external assaults upon its life, cannot be
accounted the true or just construction, however
plausibly its vindication may be attempted by literal
interpretations of particular provisions, or specious
arguments founded on the omission of others, or any
technical rules of construction, ordinarily applied to
written contracts in private life.

The nation, as history abundantly shows, *existed as
a nation before the Constitution was formed.* The
nation created the Constitution, not the Constitution
the nation. It constructed that national compact for

the more perfect definition and distribution of the various rights and powers which its citizens possessed, or were intended to possess, in their individual capacities and in their corporate capacities as States; and to establish a form of government that should be competent to protect them in the enjoyment of those rights and the exercise of those powers, and to secure to them the blessings of "a firm national government" able to protect them at home and abroad, and to preserve their national unity from destruction by foes within or foes without. And to give an instrument designed for these purposes a meaning which renders it not only powerless to accomplish them, but furnishes to enemies within the direct means of undermining and destroying *the authority* of the Government which it was designed to create and preserve, or to construe it as susceptible of any such use or abuse, or as wanting in any essential power of self-protection, is to sacrifice the substance to the form, and pervert a compact intended for the preservation of the nation's life into one for its destruction.

The Government, formed by the Constitution, represents the nation in every thing pertaining to it as a nation. Its life is the life of the nation. And it not only has the right, but is, on every principle of duty, bound, to protect that life at all costs and all hazards; and for that end to exercise other powers than those expressly given by the Constitution, if manifestly necessary for that end, upon the obvious principle that the possession of such ultimate power of self-preservation was necessarily implied in its creation.

In the language of the Report of the majority of the Committee on Reconstruction, which every one desiring to understand the subject should know by heart, —

" It is more than idle, it is a mockery, to contend that a people who have thrown off their allegiance, destroyed the local government which bound their States to the Union as members thereof, defied its authority, refused to execute its laws, and abrogated every provision which gave them political rights within the Union, shall retain, through all, the perfect and entire right to resume at their own will and pleasure all their privileges within the Union, and especially to participate in its Government, and to control the conduct of its officers. To admit such a principle for one moment would be to declare that treason is always master, and loyalty a blunder. Such a principle is void by its very nature and essence, because inconsistent with the theory of government, and fatal to its own existence."

Upon every principle, therefore, of public law applicable to a condition of peace or war; upon any reasonable construction of the Constitution in reference to the relations of the inhabitants of the several States, and of those States to the national Government which it created and defined ; and upon the fundamental principles of interpertation applicable to

civil or national compacts, — it is believed that no reasonable doubt should exist that the inhabitants of the
States recently in rebellion, by that act forfeited,
abandoned, or lost their political rights or representation in Congress, and at the close of it, by their enforced surrender, were, in the language of that report,
" disorganized communities, without civil government,
and without constitutions, or other forms by virtue
of which political relations could legally exist between them and the Federal Government." The
vast majority of them were criminals who had violated their allegiance, forfeited all rights civil or political, including those of liberty and life itself, holding
them only at the mercy of the Government which
they had thus outraged and defied, but to whose power
they had been compelled unwillingly to submit.

And consequently that they could be re-instated in
their political rights only by the assent of the Government which represented the nation, and is fully
empowered to do all things needful for the preservation of the Constitution and the Union, and the restoration of the people to unity and the enjoyment of
political privileges under them.

PART SECOND.

CHAPTER I.

REPLY TO THEORIES AND ARGUMENTS ADDUCED IN
SUPPORT OF THE PRESIDENT'S POLICY.—ALLEGED
DESTRUCTION OF STATES BY IMPOSING CONDITIONS
OF RESTORATION.

IT having been attempted, in the previous article
upon this subject, to maintain affirmatively the right
of Congress to impose upon the people of the rebel
States terms or conditions of restoration to their
political power and privileges as States in the Union
under the Constitution, a just treatment of the subject demands consideration also of the position
taken, and arguments adduced, in defence of the
opposite theory, usually designated as the President's
policy.

These are to be found in the Report of the minority of the Reconstruction Committee, the Address of
the Philadelphia Convention of August, and the
recently published letter of a gentleman, of national
celebrity as a lawyer, whose acknowledged claims to

general confidence and respect give very great weight
to his opinions upon a subject like the present, and
invest them with much of the force of judicial
authority.

The principal positions and arguments contained
in the Report and Address referred to, it is believed,
have been substantially met and answered by those
taken in the preceding article, maintaining the right
of Congress to impose such terms and conditions, —
the antagonism between them being so direct and
obvious as to render those on either side subversive
of those on the other, according to the convictions
produced in the mind of the reader ; although some
of them will receive further consideration below.
The letter, however, referred to as containing an able
epitome or summary of the whole matter, with some
new and original views, — and as having great and
wide influence in this vicinity, if not far beyond it, —
seems to demand a more careful and direct answer.

There would be several reasons which might prevent the writer of this article from entering upon the
task, if such answer were to be taken alone, as a
reply merely to that letter, and thus to place him in
seeming voluntary antagonism to a personal friend.
But personal reasons can no longer control when
such reply becomes an unavoidable duty, as a necessary portion of a humble effort to defend or uphold
a principle of government which he deems essential
to the salvation of his country from despotism or

anarchy, to the brink of which he sadly but profoundly believes her to be now brought by the course
pursued by the national Executive.

The object of the letter is to sustain the President
in the theory he has adopted, that the inhabitants of
the States recently in rebellion (and which for brevity
will be denominated "the rebel States") are lawfully
entitled to the immediate restoration of their former
political rights and powers in the administration of
the national Government, upon the determination or
fiat of the executive head of the Government that
the rebellion has ceased, and that the authority
of the Constitution and the laws of the United States
have been re-established among them; and to overthrow the contrary doctrine maintained by Congress,
that the Government, in its legislative capacity, alone
has the right and power of determining when such
restoration shall take place, and of prescribing such
terms and conditions of it as may be deemed necessary for the protection and future peace and security
of the country.

Starting with seemingly very simple postulates or
propositions, — so simple, indeed, as to have the
appearance of mere truisms, but which, it is believed,
have no substantial application to the case in
hand, — the letter proceeds to draw from them the
desired conclusions; and, having accomplished this by
way of general argument, it finally startles us with a
novel and specious construction of the Constitution,

investing the President with the omnipotent authority
he claims, — a construction believed to be entirely
original, and which, if maintainable, entitles the
author to the profound gratitude of that functionary,
and of all worshippers of the " one-man power." So
that, after the perusal of the letter in the usual manner in which papers of this sort are read, one might
naturally lay it down in a sort of dreamy conviction
that the President's policy is vindicated by the
simplest and clearest of demonstrations, " which he
who runs may read."

It is proposed, however, more carefully to examine
the premises, and the conclusions justly deducible
from them, if they can be applied to the existing
facts. And, upon such examination, it is believed
that the author of the letter, and Congress, will be
found to be much nearer to each other in ultimate
opinion, as founded upon general principles, than he
seems to imagine: and that the great difference
between them will rest mainly on the novel construction of the Constitution alluded to, which will also be
examined, and with great confidence that it has no
solid foundation.

Before proceeding, however, to these matters, it
may be well here to record two most essential principles conceded by the author, lying at the foundation of the position taken by Congress, and which, in
a justly comprehensive application of them, it is
thought go very far (if not entirely) to overthrow

the argument he has attempted to raise upon the postulates referred to.

The first is that of the unquestionable authority and right of the Government to subdue the rebellion by force of arms, laid down in these words: —

"The Government of the United States may and must, in the discharge of its constitutional duty, subdue by arms any number of its rebellious citizens into quiet submission to its lawful authority. And if the officers of a State, having the actual control of its Government, have disobeyed the requirements to swear to support the Constitution, and have abused the powers of the State, by making war on the United States, this presents the case of an usurping and unlawful Government of a State, which the United States *may lawfully destroy by force;* for, undoubtedly, the provision of the Constitution, that the United States shall guarantee to every State in this Union a republican form of government, must mean a republican form in harmony with the Constitution, and *which is so organized as to be in the Union.*" [1]

The second, and of no less importance, is that the Government of the United States alone has the power to decide when the time has come for the restoration of the inhabitants of the rebel States to their political rights and powers as States in the Union. This principle is thus laid down: —

"And if the preservation of the States within the Union was one of the objects of the war, and they can be preserved only by having republican governments organized in harmony with the Constitution, and such government can be organized only by the people of those States, then, manifestly, it is not only the right, but the constitutional duty, of the people of those States to organize

---

[1] All italicizing is by the writer of this article, unless it be otherwise stated.

10

such governments, and the Government of the United States can have no rightful authority to prohibit their organization. But *this right and duty of the people of the several States can only begin when war has ceased, and the authority of the Constitution and the laws of the United States has been restored and established; and, from the nature of the case, the Government of the United States must determine when that time has come.*"

Now, these two propositions embrace substantially all that is claimed by Congress and its supporters; the question "when the war has ceased, and the authority of the Constitution and the laws of the United States has been restored and established," — being, as is at once perceived, of very broad scope, — comprehending other most material considerations besides those of the mere laying-down of arms and formal submission to that authority.

The war cannot, with any pretence of reason, be considered to have ceased, nor the authority of the Constitution and the laws to have been restored and established, if the surrender and professed submission were formal merely, or intended to endure only so long as their enforcement could not be successfully opposed; nor if future resistance were designed of any kind; nor so long as the rights and privileges of all citizens of the United States under the Constitution and the laws could not be fully vindicated and secured by the impartial and faithful administration of justice in the courts of those States and of the United States. And, if it is lawful and just to withhold from these States the restoration of political rights and power in the administration of the national Government until these ends shall have been accomplished (as is thus conceded), it is not perceived why it may not be equally lawful and just to propose and require of them the fulfilment of reasonable conditions, by which such restoration may safely be made immediate. If the people of those States prefer the delay to accepting of the conditions, it is their own choice, and they can have no just cause of complaint.

From these two principles or propositions above cited, and the further one stated in the letter, that the only rightful objects of the war —

"are not the destruction of one or more States, but their preservation ; not the destruction of the Government in a State, *but the restoration of its government to a republican form of government in harmony with the Constitution,"* —

the further conclusion is logically inevitable, that during the rebellion, and until such re-organization, the inhabitants of those States did not compose States in the Union under the Constitution, and were not entitled to any political power and privileges as such ; although such inhabitants continued to be within the Union as citizens of the United States, and subject to the authority of the national Government. And upon these three concessions or postulates, — namely, that the Government of these United States might rightfully subdue the people of the States in rebellion by force of arms; that such people during the rebellion, and until the authority of the Constitution and the laws was restored and established, did not compose States under the Constitution, and had no right nor power to organize themselves into such States; and that the Government of the United States is the rightful judge of the time when such authority has been restored and established, and such re-organization may take place, — it is believed that the claims of Congress might safely be rested, as substantially controlling all the other positions taken in the letter, saving that of the new construction above alluded to.

But the specious logic of the letter requires, perhaps, a more critical examination of the premises and mode of argument adopted in defence of the President's policy, and in opposition to the claims of Congress.

Of the premises or postulates, the first in order is in these words:—

"The nature of our Government does not permit the United States to destroy a State, or acquire its territory by conquest."

The second is as follows : —

"Neither does it permit the people of a State to destroy the State, or lawfully affect in any way any one of its relations to the United States."

And both are said to be equally inconsistent with the Constitution. In another place, the first premise is stated thus: —

"But neither the power and duty of the Government of the

United States to subdue by arms rebellious people in the territorial limits of one or more States, nor its power and duty to destroy a usurping Government *de facto*, can possibly authorize the United States to destroy one of the States of the Union, or, *what must amount to the same thing, to acquire that absolute right over its people and its territory which results from conquest in a foreign war.*"

Now, these premises, taken in their literal and seemingly natural meaning, are simple and undeniable, excepting the assertion that to exercise the rights of conquest over the inhabitants of a rebellious State, subdued by force of arms of the Government of the United States, is the same thing as the destruction of the State by that Government, which will presently be considered. No one ever pretended that the Government of the United States, acting within its constitutional limits, could voluntarily destroy a State, or could voluntarily assent to the withdrawal of a State from the Union, or to the alteration of any of her constitutional relations to it. And, if these premises are to be thus understood, it is obvious that they have no relevancy to the case under consideration. But it is impossible to believe this to be their intended signification. To give to them any reasonable interpretation, as applicable to any issue before the country, they must be construed as implying and intended to signify, that any terms imposed upon the people of the rebel States as conditions of their restoration to the privileges of States in the Union, beyond those of present submission to the authority of

the Constitution and the laws, is virtually the destruction of those States, or can be rightfully enforced
only upon the hypothesis that the Government of the
United States has accomplished that destruction by
becoming their conquerors in war.

This mode of reasoning, usually founded by its authors on representations or implications that the Government was the aggressor which inaugurated the
war, and was pursuing it for the conquest of the rebel
States and their subjugation to its authority, — and
which gives a corresponding bias to all their arguments and hypotheses, — however unconsciously
adopted, is nevertheless believed to be founded upon
an entire misconception or erroneous supposition of
the facts as really existing, not to say on one the
entire reverse of the truth.

No one can honestly deny, that the war was originally inaugurated, declared, and carried on by the
people of the rebel States in pursuance of a long-
cherished design to dismember the Government of the
United States, to destroy the Union, and to erect a
huge Southern slave empire on a portion of its ruins;
and that the Government of the United States, from
the beginning to the end of it, was acting purely and
solely on the defensive, to save itself and the Union
from destruction, according to the duty imposed upon
it by the Constitution ; and that so far from its having been instrumental in the destruction of those
States, or of any of their relations to the Union, or

seeking any such destruction, its sole object has been
to save them from it.

It is true, that their relations to the Union, as
States under the Constitution, have been destroyed.
But that destruction was the work of their own hands,
not that of the national Government. It was they
who, repudiating the Constitution and authority of
the United States, abolishing their former governments established under them, sundering all the
relations which could constitute them States in the
Union, and establishing a foreign and hostile government, waged open war upon the Government of the
United States to accomplish its destruction. And is
it not, in the face of these facts, a marvellous perversion to talk of them as being destroyed, or of
their destruction as being sought by that government?
Or to say that any thing which the Government has
done, is doing, or can do, renders it in any degree
accountable for their destruction? Is it not undeniable, that they themselves, alone, have been guilty of
the most criminal *self-destruction* as States under the
Constitution? that they have died by their own hands,
and not by the hands of the United States? and that
all which is left for the United States to do is to aid
in their resurrection from the graves dug by themselves?

It is in the light of these facts that we are to judge
of the justness of the position above referred to ;
namely, that for the Government of the United States

to acquire that absolute right over the people of a State and its territory which results from conquests in a foreign war is the same thing as to destroy the State. This word " State," as used in this connection, in order to have any sensible meaning, must be construed to mean a State under the Constitution, and preserving its constitutional relations to the Union. And how, after the people of it have themselves destroyed it, and the Government has conquered them in a long and bloody war, the exercise of any rights of conquest in order to compel them to return to their allegiance, or to make it secure from future violation, is the same thing as destroying it, is not clear to every comprehension. If it was already destroyed, as such a State, by its own people, the rights of conquest could add nothing to such destruction, however exercised ; and surely not, if exercised solely for its restoration.

These premises therefore, it is believed, may be laid aside as being either irrelevant to any question in issue, or, if susceptible of any seeming relevancy, being so only upon the assumption or supposition of facts having no existence.

CHAPTER II.

ASSERTED CONSTITUTIONAL LIMITS TO POWERS OF CON-
GRESS.—THEORY THAT THE PEOPLE OF THE LATE
REBEL STATES ARE ENTITLED TO COMPLETE IMME-
DIATE RESTORATION.

BUT the position doubtless mainly relied upon in
denial of the right of Congress to enforce any terms
upon the inhabitants of the rebel States as conditions of restoration, is, that the right of the Government of the United States to subdue the rebellion
was a *constitutional right*, which can be lawfully exercised only " *within the limits of the powers conferred by the Constitution;*" and that this right is
thus confined to the subjugation of the rebellion, and
the restoration and establishment of the authority of
the Constitution and the laws of the United States
in the rebellious territories; and that, when such
restoration and establishment have taken place,—by
whatever means,—the inhabitants *become ipso facto,
as matter of right*, entitled to re-organization as States
under the Constitution, and to the immediate enjoyment of their former political powers and privileges
conferred by it; and hence, that no terms of indemnity for the past or security for the future, however

11

mild or generous, or however reasonable, can be exacted.

Now, admitting the theory to be true that the right of the Government to subdue the rebellion was a strictly constitutional right, and to be exercised solely for the purpose of restoring and re-establishing the authority of the Constitution and the laws in the rebel States, and of bringing them into the fold of the Union, — it is not perceived where any limits are prescribed by the Constitution, or by what course of reasoning any can be inferred from it, which prohibit the Government, after the rightful subjugation of its rebellious subjects by force of arms, from requiring of them indemnity for the injuries they have inflicted upon the nation, so far as such indemnity is possible ; or from prescribing such conditions of restoration to their former political powers and privileges as may be necessary to prevent the future perversion of them to the like criminal purposes ; and such security for the personal safety, freedom, and immunities of all citizens of the United States within their borders as justice, humanity, and the plighted faith of the Government, make necessary.

If the Government has the constitutional right to subdue its rebellious subjects by war for the purpose of restoring the authority of the Constitution and the laws over them, it follows in the plainest logical necessity that it must have also the constitutional right to make that restoration complete and permanent; for otherwise it can in no just sense be accounted a full restoration. And as the Constitution neither does nor could prescribe limits to the exercise of the military power necessary for the purposes of such subjugation and restoration, so neither does it, nor could it, prescribe limits to the power by which they shall be rendered permanently secure. Both must be left to the good faith and sound discretion of the Government, applied to the exigencies as they arise. And it is conceded on all hands that it alone must be the judge to decide when such restoration shall be accounted as accomplished.

It is believed that the case on this point might be very safely rested here, as showing that upon the principles affirmed or conceded by the author of the letter, carried out to their legitimate issues, the Government has an unquestionable right to prescribe such terms as, in the exercise of good faith and a sound discretion, it should see fit to impose as conditions of the restoration of the people of the rebel States to their former political powers and privileges. But the theory of their immediate right to such restoration without any conditions or limitations whatever, which he asserts and attempts to maintain, appears to be so utterly inconsistent with any reasonable appreciation of the facts as known to exist, and to lead to consequences so seemingly subversive of all future peace and security, that they cannot be suffered to pass unnoticed. He states this theory in these remarkable words : —

"After much reflection, and with no such partiality for executive power as would be likely to lead one astray, I have formed
the opinion that the Southern States are *now as rightfully, and
should be as effectively, in the Union* as they were before the mad-
ness of their people attempted to carry them out of it; and in this
opinion I believe a majority of the people of the United States
agree."

It is presumed, that, by this time, the author must •
be convinced that a very great majority of the people
of the Northern States entertain a totally contrary
opinion. And if, from the votes cast in the late elec-
tions, those of interested office-seekers and their
friends, of sympathizers in the rebellion from the
start to this hour, of hirelings paid for their ballots,
of those actuated by an unrelenting hatred of the
Republican party as a controlling motive, and of
the hordes of ignorant foreigners who constitute the
strength of the Democratic party in the great cities,
were to be stricken out of the count, he would, it
is believed, find himself in a minority, in point of
numbers, indeed most miserable.

But how does this theory comport with the facts?
It is undeniable, in view of all the evidence before the
the world, — in the report of the Committee upon
Reconstruction; in the daily reports from Southern
newspapers; in the public speeches and addresses
of the leading men of the South, both occasional and
official; in the action of their legislatures and so-
called courts of justice; in the reports of the
military commanders stationed among them, **and** of

the officers of the Freedmen's Bureau; in the
multitudinous relations of murders and outrages upon
the black man; and in accounts of the insecurity
of life in many parts of the Southern States, to any
Union man out of the scope of military protection,
with which the daily papers and private letters are
• filled, — in the view of all this evidence, and with the
ghastly massacres of Memphis and New Orleans
yet fresh in remembrance, it is undeniable that a
general and almost universal conviction prevails at
this moment, among the inhabitants of the rebel
States, that their cause was a just one; that the
undertaking, on the part of the Government of the
United States, to subdue them was unrighteous and
cruel, and that they are the victims of oppression by
the mere fortunes of war; that the debt incurred by
them was in defence of their sacred rights, and ought
to be conscientiously paid; that the debt contracted
by the United States was the fruit of an unjustifiable
and wicked war upon them, and should be repudiated, or at least that no portion of it should be
assessed upon them; that slavery, which they were
forced to abolish, was in truth a divine institution, the
best possible for the black man as well as for the
white; that the security and happiness of both races
require that the negro should be held in perpetual
subordination, as the hewer of wood and drawer of
water; that the privilege of the ballot, of serving as
a juror, or of holding any office of honor or emolu-

ment, or of owning or hiring land, or of education, are all alike inconsistent with the dignity and safety of the white man, or the real good of the black man; and that, if any opportunity should hereafter present itself for them to re-assert their right of secession, and establish a Southern empire, it would be perfectly righteous for them to do so.

Such are unquestionably the temper, the feelings, the sentiments, and opinions of the great majority of Southern men and women at this time, and of nearly all of their recognized leaders. If, then, the authority of the Constitution and the laws of the United States is, or appears to be, so far established among them, that its courts and magistrates of law and other officers are permitted to re-assume their functions, and no open or organized resistance of it is ventured upon, they nevertheless all stand upon the ashes of this smothered volcano, whose embers are still burning with intense heat beneath them, and where existing forms of law and government are notoriously inadequate for the security of the lives and liberty of the freedmen, who lie exposed to the merciless inflictions of State legislation, and the still more merciless persecutions of vindictive social hatred, from which nothing in the existing Constitution and laws can protect them.

This seeming restoration, then, of the authority of the Constitution and the laws, if, indeed, such seeming can be said to exist, is but an outward show;

and, while the heart of the South remains unchanged, can be but a hollow truce, unless some fitting safeguard for the future be erected. Nor can it be justly said that such precautions would indicate unjust and unworthy suspicions of the good faith of the inhabitants of the Southern States, who have professedly returned to their allegiance. The difficulty is not in supposing them less worthy of trust than other men, or than the people of the North might be in the like circumstances. It is in the nature of man, that he cannot long and patiently submit in silence and quiet under the sense of such accumulated wrong and injustice as the people of the South imagine to be thus heaped upon them. And, if the smothered fire should not find vent in another open outbreak, it inevitably must in the secret windings of political machinations and combinations tending to the same end. Some security, therefore, seems indispensable for the preservation of any future peace or permament safety of the Union.

But why, it is asked, is not the new oath of allegiance sufficient, and all that can be reasonably demanded of honorable men or good citizens? The answer is obvious. Nearly all the leading men of the South had taken the oath of allegiance to the United States, and broke it unhesitatingly to take part in the rebellion, and substitute a new oath of allegiance to another and hostile government. And they did this, they say, conscientiously, under the

conviction that allegiance was primarily due to their
respective States, and that the allegiance due to the
United States was secondary only. And in this view
they were and are sustained by the nearly unanimous
voice of their people. And, they still earnestly maintain that they were right in this construction of their
duties, and spurn with indignation the imputation of
any treason or falsehood against the Government of
the United States. And, this being so, what security
can there be that this new oath will not be taken or
construed with the like mental reservation? or, if that
might not be, why might they not hereafter, and with
truth, assert that this oath was not voluntary, but one
extorted under duress and the force of arms, and
therefore not binding upon the conscience?

In view, therefore, of the facts, and of the general
principles to be applied to them, it seems to follow,
as of logical necessity, that (however the powers of
the Government of the United States might be supposed to be otherwise limited by the Constitution, in
the carrying-on of the war and in prescribing conditions of peace and restoration) whatever terms are
demanded by the exigency, in order to make such
peace and restoration entire and permanent, must be
within the scope of those powers; and that some
such terms or conditions are imperatively demanded
in the present case.

Upon what reason or principle, then, is this doctrine
denied, and an attempt made to show that the Consti-

tution does interpose to limit those powers and to
prevent the imposition of any such terms?

The main argument, if argument it may be called,
seems to consist in the formula above cited; namely,
that the right of the Government to subdue the rebellion, being a constitutional right, could be exercised only "within the limits of the powers conferred
by the Constitution;" that those powers, being confined to the restoration and re-establishment of the
authority of the Constitution and the laws in the rebellious States, were exhausted when such restoration
and establishment were accomplished, and the people of those States therefore become entitled to immediate restoration of all their former political
powers and privileges in the Union; and therefore
that an attempt to impose upon them any terms or
conditions of such restoration is an usurpation, having no other foundation than the assumed right of
the conqueror to dictate terms of peace, and which
right, it is alleged, pertains to conquest in a foreign
war only, and not to one in a civil war. And no
little dust has been thrown into the eyes of the
public, by efforts to make it appear that Congress,
in undertaking to impose any terms or conditions
of restoration, are usurping, and assuming to act
upon, the rights and powers of conquerors in a
foreign war.

It must be apparent to every reader, that this style
of reasoning is founded upon an entire begging of

12

the whole question: first, in assuming that the rebels, upon such submission, became immediately and unconditionally entitled to enjoyment of their former powers and privileges in the Union,—when the main question at issue is whether they do become so; and, secondly, in assuming that the right of the conqueror in war to dictate terms of peace is confined exclusively to foreign war, and does not extend to civil war,—which is also one of the material questions to be decided.

In reference to the first of these questions, it is believed that no further argument can be needed to prove that the right of the Government to subdue the rebellion, and restore the authority of the Constitution and the laws in the rebellious States, involves, by an inevitable logical necessity, the right to impose upon the people of those States such terms and conditions as shall make such restoration secure and permanent, or to hold them under its military authority until it shall have become so.

CHAPTER III.

RIGHT OF GOVERNMENT AS CONQUEROR TO DICTATE TERMS OF PEACE.

In discussing the right of the Government to dictate terms and conditions of peace as the victors in the struggle, we must put aside, as wholly irrelevant, all questions concerning the right of the Government of the United States to hold the inhabitants of territories, acquired by conquest in a foreign war, permanently under military control, or under territorial or colonial administration only; or of its obligation to admit them into the Union as States when fitted for such admission. Also, any question of its right or power, as the conqueror, to hold the inhabitants of the rebel States in permanent military or other control as territories or colonies; or to impose upon them any terms or conditions of restoration to their former political rights and powers, which it may see fit to impose in the exercise of its arbitrary will only, without due regard to such ultimate restoration. And with them may go the nonsensical clamor about military usurpation, military despotism, despotic will, and irresponsible power, heaped upon Congress for maintaining its right, as the victor, to impose conditions of peace.

It is conceded, that the nature of the Government of the United States, as created by the Constitution, does limit its powers, as conquerors of the rebel States, to the effectual subjugation of their inhabitants to its authority, for the purpose of the restoration of them to their former rights and privileges as States in the Union; and would not allow it to hold them in permanent arbitrary subjection, as conquered territories merely, any longer than may be needful for the accomplishment of such restoration. But it is maintained that the Government, nevertheless, has full right and power, as the conqueror in the war, to prescribe the terms and conditions of peace upon which such restoration shall be granted, unlimited and unshackled by any provisions of the Constitution, or any other restraints than those of obedience to humanity, justice, sound national policy, and the preservation of the Union; and that the Constitution does not expressly, nor by implication, interpose to shield the inhabitants of those States from the imposition of such terms and conditions, or to entitle them to reassume their participation of power in the national councils, free from all restraint upon its perversion for accomplishing hereafter the same purposes which they sought to gain in the field. Any other principle obviously deprives the Government, whose life is the life of the nation, of the power of self-preservation, and makes the Constitution, which created it, the ready means for its destruction.

The truth is manifest, that the exigency of a civil war, by a combination of States against the General Government, was not anticipated by the framers of the Constitution, and is nowhere contemplated in its provisions; and consequently that the terms of it have nothing to do with the case in hand, further than this: that in establishing a frame of government upon the broadest principles of freedom and humanity, and for the especial purpose of establishing and perpetuating the Union, they impose upon that government corresponding obligations to treat rebellious subjects with all the mercy and magnanimity which the nature of their crime and the safety of the republic will allow; and the further sacred duty of preserving the Union unimpaired, by restoring the rebel States to their former places in it, as soon as such restoration can be safely accomplished; but leaving the time and mode of discharging these duties to the exercise of its judgment and discretion, to be faithfully exercised for the good of the whole nation. The common sense of the people of the United States, of mankind, and of history will repudiate as absurd any hypothesis that the Constitution imposes any other limits to the authority of the national Government in such an exigency, or binds any such fetters about its limbs as render it incapable of self-defence, or of saving the nation for whose preservation it was created.

As the Constitution, in investing the Government
with the power to enter upon foreign war, impliedly
clothed it with all the rights incident to conquest,
including that of dictating the terms of peace, and
unlimited by any other restraints than those imposed
by the nature of the Government and the objects of
the war; so, in investing it with the power to subdue
rebellious subjects in a civil war, it gives the like
right to impose the terms and conditions of peace, or,
which is the same thing, of restoration to their
former rights and privileges, unlimited by any other
than the like restraints. The reason is the same in
both cases. This right of the conqueror is not founded upon any arbitrary rule, nor is it any merely
gratuitous prerogative granted to the strongest as
the fruit of victory, but rests upon the absolute
and unavoidable necessity of the case, there being
no common arbiter or judge who can decide between the parties upon the reasonableness or justice
of the terms upon which peace should be made; and
which necessity is as absolute in a civil war as in a
foreign war.

In considering the applicability of the rule in this
instance, it must be conceded that if there ever was
a case, or one could be imagined, in which a civil
war could or should vest in the victorious Government
all the rights of the conqueror as in a foreign war,
this is most emphatically that case; for whether regarded in reference to the acknowledged absence of

any justifying cause for the rebellion, or to the extent of national territory held for four years in exclusive and hostile array against the national forces, or to the worse than barbaric ill faith and fiendish cruelty with which the war on their part was waged, or to the enormous sacrifices of precious life and countless treasure which it cost, the enormity of the crime against civilization and humanity has no parallel, and no punishment could exceed that due to the guilty authors of it. Justice and humanity, as well as national policy, would alike dictate, that, at the close of the struggle, they should lie at the feet of their victors.

The entire identity of the rights and powers incident to victory in civil war with those of victory in foreign war is broadly and clearly laid down in the elementary writers on public law of the highest authority. It is so necessary to have this material element in the argument immediately before the reader, that no other apology is necessary for repeating the citation from Vattel above made in another connection. He states the principle thus : —

"A civil war breaks the bands of society and government, or at least suspends their force and effect. It produces in the nation two independent parties, who consider each other as enemies, and *acknowledge no common judge.* These two parties, therefore, must necessarily be considered as constituting, at least for a time, two separate bodies, two distinct societies. Having no common superior to judge between them, *they stand in precisely the same predicament as two nations who engage in a contest, and have recourse to arms.*"

Wheaton lays down the law thus : —

"The general usage of nations regards such a war (civil war) as entitling both the contending parties to all the rights of war as against each other, and even as respects neutral nations." (Wheaton's International Law, Dana's ed., § 296.)

Mr. Dana annexes a very elaborate note upon the subject of belligerent rights incident to civil war, both in regard to the parties to it and to foreign nations, but suggests no distinction between the rights of victory in that and those of victory in a foreign war. And it is believed that no such distinction is anywhere intimated by any writer upon public law. If it had been, it could not have escaped this learned and thorough master of the subject. It seems impossible to believe, that, if the broad difference contended for were contemplated by them as having legal existence, they should never have made allusion to it; and equally incredible, that, if founded on any sound principle, it should not have occurred to their minds. So far, therefore, as their opinions may be inferred both from their language and their silence, it is believed that they may be considered as rejecting any such distinction.

And the reason of the case is manifestly against any. The fundamental principles of the right of the victor to prescribe the terms of peace in a foreign war, apply, not only with equal, but with greater force, in a civil war. That of the necessity of the case, namely, because there can be no common arbiter or judge between them, is of equal validity in both cases. And, in reference to qualifications of the arbiter, who but the victorious Government can decide upon the nature or degree of the crime involved in the treason, the punishment justly due, the amount of injuries for which indemnity may justly be demanded, the security necessary to guard against future like revolt, or for the protection of the lives, liberties, rights, and property of the loyal citizens of the Union in the territories of the rebel States, and the other questions necessarily involved in any adjustment of the terms of peace?

It is absurd to pretend, that, upon the surrender of the rebel forces and the cessation of opposition to the authority of the Constitution and the laws, the Constitution becomes the arbiter ; for the whole question is of the right of the rebels to be restored to any privileges under it, or of the terms upon which such restoration shall be made ; and, until that shall have been completed. their constitutional rights are the subject in dispute, not the arbiter by which it can be decided.

Again, the rule applies to the case of a civil war with much greater reason, from the consideration, that in such a war, where the legitimate Government has succeeded in subduing an unrighteous rebellion, the conquered are malefactors, guilty of the highest crime known in civilized society, and the terms of whose pardon, therefore, upon all the principles

and analogies of law, rest of right in the sense of justice and humanity of the Government whose authority
they have spurned, and whose laws they have outraged.

What, then, are the reasons urged in denial of this
right? So far as they can be gathered from this letter, and the minority Report, and other publications,
they are thus related : —

" When the war has ceased, when the authority of the Constitution and laws of the United States have been restored and established, the United States are in possession, not under a new title as
conquerors, but under their old title as the lawful Government of
the country ; that title has been vindicated, not by the destruction
of one or more States, but by their preservation, and this preservation can only be entered into by the restoration of republican governments organized in harmony with the Constitution."

" Conquest of a foreign country gives absolute unlimited sovereign rights ; but no nation ever makes such a conquest of its own
territory. If a hostile power, either from without or within, takes
and holds possession and dominion over any portion of its territory,
and the nation by force of arms expel or overthrow the enemy, and
suppress hostilities, it acquires no new title, and merely regains the
possession of that of which it was temporarily deprived. The nation acquires no new sovereignty, but merely maintains its previous
rights."

" When the United States take possession of a rebel district, they
merely vindicate their pre-existing title. Under despotic governments, confiscation may be unlimited : but, under our Government,
the right of sovereignty over any portion of a State is given and
limited by the Constitution, and will be the same after the war as
before."

Now, in regard to these positions, it may be said in
the first place, as above stated, that the war cannot be

said to be ended, and the authority of the Constitution
and the laws to be restored and established, so long
as military power is necessary to maintain it, as is
now the case in large portions of the Southern States;
nor while such restoration is merely formal, tempo-
rary, or insecure; nor until it shall be made complete
by suitable safeguards prescribed as the terms of
peace: and in the second place, as before shown,
that no one pretends that the nature of our Government would allow any retention of the territories of
the rebel States as conquered foreign territory, subject to despotic authority or military power only, if
the inhabitants were willing to return to their allegiance, under such terms as justice and humanity, and
the national safety, demand. All that is maintained
is, that, until such return and restoration, the Government has full right, as the conqueror, to prescribe
those terms, unlimited by any provisions contained
in the Constitution; and that the Constitution can
have no application to any question concerning any
rights of the rebels until the final restoration of its
authority over them, upon such conditions as the
Government shall have imposed, and they shall have
accepted.

It is undoubtedly true, that the Government, upon
the subjugation of the armies of the rebels and resumption of possession of their territories, has acquired no new title, but is in such possession by virtue of the old one. And the result would be the same,

if, instead of the hostile possession taken by the rebels, it had been one taken by a foreign invading enemy. No one can question, that, in the latter case, if the invaders were so numerous, and had been so long in possession, as to render their expulsion or extermination impossible, the Government could impose upon them such terms of permanent submission to its authority, and for protection of its loyal subjects there remaining, as it should think proper. And upon what principle can it be denied that the Government has the like right in reference to its rebellious citizens, who, far more criminal than any invaders could have been, have long held hostile possession of these territories, and from whom securities for future obedience to the Constitution and the laws, and for the protection of the loyal citizens residing among them from cruel persecution, are demanded alike by justice and humanity, and the national safety?

And if it be true, as is conceded, that the United States, upon the subjugation of the rebellion, " are in possession, not under a new title, as conquerors, but under their old title as the lawful Government of the country," it is none the less true that the Government re-assumes its sway over citizens whose condition has been radically changed by the rebellion, and with powers over them which it never before possessed. Instead of loyal subjects, entitled to perfect immunity in the rights of property, liberty, and life which it could not impair, it finds them criminals, who have forfeited all such immunity, and who stand liable to be bereft of all those blessings under the laws which they have violated. Nor can such immunity be restored to them, but by its pardoning grace, and upon such terms of submission and security for future good behavior as its sense of justice and of political expediency may dictate. And it is not perceived why, upon the same principles, the Government has not the right to impose the like terms or conditions of restoration to their former political rights and privileges in the councils of the nation.

The soundness of a theory may be best illustrated by familiar examples. That of the supposed success of England in subduing the colonies in the war of the Revolution has been already adverted to. And if, in such a case, she would have had the constitutional right (which is believed to be undeniable) of imposing such terms and conditions of restoration to the colonists, of their former political rights and privileges under their charters, as her Government might have considered to be demanded by justice and the future peace and security of the empire, what becomes of the distinction between a civil and a foreign war as to the power of the conqueror to dictate terms of peace?

But a still more satisfactory illustration may be found by applying the theory to the case in hand. That theory is, that, in subduing the rebellion, the Government of the United States can only act rightfully *within the limits of the powers conferred by the Constitution ; and that these powers are confined to the restoration of the authority of the Constitution and laws of the United States* in the rebel States ; and therefore that upon the laying-down of their arms, and the proffered and apparent submission of the rebels to such authority, they became instantly, *ipsis factis*, entitled to be re-instated in all their former political powers and privileges as States in the Union ; and that the Government has no right to interpose any such terms or conditions of such re-instatement as otherwise might be obviously reasonable and necessary for the future peace and safety of the nation, and which it might have imposed but for these limits upon its power affixed by the Constitution.

Now, this theory manifestly involves the singular doctrine, that while the rebels might carry on the war, and, if successful, might dictate terms of peace without any limits or restraints, but those of the law of nations, and their own sense of justice and humanity, — " Heaven save the mark ! " — the Government of the United States is bound, not only by these laws and its sense of right, but also hand and foot by the iron bands of the Constitution, crippling its strength in the combat, and laying it, even in victory, at the feet of the conquered, for them to assume its powers, and enter at once upon the administration of its authority.

How would the case have stood, if the rebels had

realized their hopeful anticipations of laying Philadelphia, New York, and Boston in ashes, or under
contribution; and of dictating the terms of peace
and of the future relations between the loyal States
and the newly established slave empire, which was to
control the destinies of America?

The war must have terminated, of course, as all
wars must, by a treaty of peace between the two
Governments. And it is worth while to contemplate
for a moment what would probably have been the
principal terms dictated by the victorious slave-
holders.

First, There would have been the condition that
nothing should be contained in the legislation or
jurisprudence of the conquered States derogatory to
the institution of slavery, as being of divine origin,
and as instinct with justice and humanity towards the
black man.

Second, That all the black men, women, and
children in the free States, who had ever been held
in slavery in the slave States, and had escaped or
gone into the free States under any circumstances,
and the descendants of any residing therein, should
be immediately delivered up to their former owners,
or their legal representatives; and that commissioners, of known sympathy with the institution, should
be appointed with full power to decide all questions
arising under the treaty, and to deliver up such
former slaves or their descendants, if any, to the

claimants; and to call in the aid of the sheriffs of their counties, with their *posse comitatus*, to protect the owner in possession and transportation of such slaves out of the free States.

Third, That the citizens of the Southern empire should have the right at all times to carry their slaves into the free States and the territories thereof, and use and treat them there in the same manner as they were accustomed to use and treat them in their own States, and to hire them out while there, free from all molestation by act or speech; and that any such molestation should be an offence punishable by laws to be enacted for the purpose.

Fourth, That a law should be enacted, in each of the free States, requiring the immediate arrest and imprisonment of any slave who should thereafter escape from a slave State into a free State, by any person knowing of such escape, or upon complaint of his or her owner, or of any person assuming to act in his or her behalf; and that any citizen of a free State who should knowingly, or with reasonable cause of suspicion, aid or abet any such slave in so escaping, or harbor or conceal him or her, or give to him or her any succor or relief whatsoever, or who should fail to render aid when required in the recapture and restoration of such slave, should, on conviction, be punished by a fine, say, of not less than a thousand dollars, and of imprisonment for a term not less than five years for the first offence, of ten years for the second, and with death for the third; and that all trials for any such offences should be before commissioners to be appointed as aforesaid, and without the intervention of a jury, and without appeal.

Fifth, That the United States should pay all the expenses incurred by the Confederate States in carrying on the war, and prescribed pensions to the families of all their soldiers who had died in consequence of it.

Sixth, That no memorials or other tributes of honorable remembrance should be erected in any portion of the free States of those, their children, who had fallen in the war.

Seventh, That it should be lawful for the owner of any slave escaping from either of the Confederate States into either of the United States, to pursue him in the territories thereof, and retake him by force of arms, if necessary, and transport him to the owner's place of residence, without being held guilty of any violation of the laws of neutrality, or of the laws of the State thus entered upon; and that no fortresses or fortifications should be erected by the United States upon the lines dividing the two empires, nor within fifty miles thereof.

No one can reasonably suppose that these requisitions would, in any degree, have transcended those which would have been imposed upon the people of

the loyal States, if they had been as effectually subdued as are those of the rebel States.

But now that victory has perched upon the stand-
ard of the United States, and absolute power is in
her grasp to vindicate the majesty of her outraged
laws, to demand indemnity for the enormous treasure
expended in maintaining her authority (none being
possible for the infinitely greater loss of the lives of
her children), and to require security for her peace
and safety against future like revolt, or political
machinations to accomplish the same ends, — all
demanded by the simplest justice, and free from all
taint of oppression, — we are coolly told that the
Constitution prohibits the exercise of any such powers ; that these reasonable demands are wholly unconstitutional ; that all which the Government can
lawfully do is instantly to re-instate these still unsub-
dued though conquered enemies in all their former
political rights and privileges, and admit them into
immediate participation in the administration of its
authority.

Upon this doctrine, the conclusion is obvious, that,
in such a conflict, the traitors are at all times mas-
ters of the situation, and that, if defeated, the conquered, and not the conquerors, dictate the terms of
peace.

Another logical result from this theory is, that if,
by any combination of circumstances, the inhabitants
of States desirous to secede should obtain command

of a majority in both houses of Congress, either by the numbers of their own Senators and Representatives, or by combination with corrupt members misrepresenting the loyal States, or otherwise; and upon an attempt to exercise their political power in destroying the Union, and dismembering the Government, should be resisted by the people of the loyal States by force of arms, and be effectually subdued in the field, as they now have been, — they would nevertheless have the perfect right, upon the laying-down of their arms, to resume their places in the national councils, there to resume their nefarious efforts, and again effect their purpose, or expose the nation to the horrors of civil war; and, if needful, might repeat the iniquitous game until the people of the loyal States, exhausted by successive conflicts, or weary of the strife and hopeless of repose, should be finally compelled to submit.

Such are the clearly inevitable logical results of the theory which the President has adopted, which he is pleased to style his policy, and which he proclaims to be the only one in accordance with the Constitution; upon which he seeks to replace the inhabitants of the rebel States in immediate possession of their previous political power and influence in combination with their former allies of the Northern Democracy; and by which, on his individual responsibility and in declared opposition to the will of the representatives of the people, he is perilling the present tranquillity and future safety of the country. The voice of an indignant people has already pronounced its condemnation, with an emphasis which can leave no doubt either of its merits or of its fate.

CHAPTER IV.

ASSERTED POWERS OF THE PRESIDENT, AS THE EXECUTIVE HEAD OF THE GOVERNMENT AND AS COMMANDER-IN-CHIEF, TO DECIDE UPON THE RIGHTS OF THE REBEL STATES TO IMMEDIATE RESTORATION.

It remains only to consider the novel and remarkable construction of the Constitution, above mentioned, upon which the President's policy is attempted to be sustained by the author of the letter. It is thus stated: —

"The question whether *de facto* governments and hostile populations have been completely subdued by arms, and the lawful authority of the United States restored and re-established, *is a military and executive question.* It does not require legislative action to ascertain the necessary facts; and, from the nature of the case, legislative action cannot change or materially affect them. As commander-in-chief of the army and navy, and as the chief executive officer whose constitutional duty it is to see that the laws are faithfully executed, it is the official duty of the President to know whether a rebellion has been suppressed, and whether the authority of the Constitution and laws of the United States has been completely restored and firmly established. The mere organization of a republican government in harmony with the Union, by the people of one of the existing States of the United States, requires no enabling act of Congress, and I can find no authority in the Constitution for any interference by Congress to prohibit or regulate the organization of such a government by the people of an existing State of the Union: on the other hand, it is clearly necessary that the President should act so far at least as to remove out of the way military restrictions on the power of the people to assemble and do those acts which are necessary to re-organize their government. This I think he was bound to do as soon as he became satisfied that the right time had come."

It would be difficult to exaggerate the alarming and dangerous nature of this doctrine, if it could be successfully maintained. It might well startle the nation to find that the power of final decision upon the relations subsisting between the inhabitants of the rebel States and the national Government, and between them and the other States in the Union, growing out of such a gigantic civil war as that through which we are passing, and the adjustment of which relations must vitally affect the nature, the safety, and the strength of that Government for ages to come, if not for ever, rests wholly in one individual; and that the representatives of the people are voiceless and powerless to control or affect it.

No one can believe that power of such tremendous import would ever have been intentionally vested in the executive head of the Government alone, by the framers of the Constitution, if the exigency had been foreseen. No one will believe that it would have been conferred by the people even upon a Washington or a Lincoln, or that either of them would voluntarily have assumed it. It is a power from which it would seem that any man, the most reckless of responsibility, would naturally shrink, if having only his country's good at heart; gladly turning for

advice and assistance to the representative agents of
the people, instead of repelling them with vitupera-
tion and insult for questioning his supremacy.

The first obvious comment to be made upon this
theory is, that it rests entirely upon the assumption,
or the hypothesis attempted to be maintained in the
former part of the letter, that the people of the
rebel States, upon outward submission to the authority of the Constitution and the laws of the United
States, became instantly entitled to the restoration of
their former political powers and privileges in the
Union; and that the Government was prohibited or
disabled by the Constitution from exacting any indemnity, or requiring any security for their future
continued obedience, or any guarantees for the peace
and safety of the nation, however reasonable or just
such demands might otherwise be considered. It
merely transfers the right of decision of the *question
of such submission* from the General Government
to the Executive Department alone. If, therefore,
that hypothesis is unsound, — as it is believed most
clearly to be, as above shown, — this new theory of
construction of course falls to the ground with it.
For the most extreme defender of the President's
policy would not venture to affirm, that, if any terms,
conditions, or guarantees could be lawfully demanded,
he would have any right or power to determine their
nature or extent.

Before proceeding to consider the various reasons

which are believed sufficient to prove this theory to be wholly untenable, it is necessary to have a clear and distinct understanding of the two elements or principles upon which alone it is made to rest; namely, the executive power and the military power of the President. These two powers, although often, as in this case, confounded together, as jointly conferring authority which neither singly could give, are totally distinct and independent, and are utterly unsusceptible of any fusion or commingling, so as to produce a result which neither could alone effect. And, if the authority claimed for the President cannot be deduced from either taken singly, it cannot be from the two combined. Two ciphers cannot make a unit nor can any multiplication of them.

Now, nothing in political science or language, and nothing indeed in common conversation, is better defined or more universally recognized than the meaning of the term "executive" as applied to government. Every one knows that it is descriptive of the head of the civil Government, who *executes the laws*, as distinguished from the legislature which enacts them, and the judiciary which applies them; and that it designates an exclusively civil power for the execution of civil laws. It is equally clear and universally known, that *military officers form no part of the government, but are its instruments only* for especial purposes, and are never termed " the Executive" nor " executive officers;" and that military authority is no constituent part of the Government, but merely an agency by which it discharges certain of its duties or functions. The term "executive" is a correlative term, always used in correlation to "judicial" and "legislative," and never as having any reference to military authority. All dictionaries and encyclopædias, as well as common usage, are perfectly co-incident on this point.

It is true, that the Constitution (Art. II., Sec. 1), after providing that "the executive power shall be vested in the President of the United States of America," and prescribing the manner of his election, qualifications, &c., provides in another section (Sec. 2) that "the President shall be commander-in-chief of the army and navy of the United States, and of the militia of the several States when called into the actual service of the United States." But this neither creates nor implies any expansion of his "executive power," but is merely the annexation to his civil office of another entirely distinct and different one. There was no necessity, in the nature of things, for investing him with this military authority as part of his powers as the head of the civil Government. And if the Constitution had provided that the commander-in-chief should be any other person, and appointed in any other manner, it would have derogated nothing from the President's executive supremacy; nor can such addition of military to executive authority render acts done under it executive acts,

15

any more than would the investment of the Chief
Justice with the command of the army and navy render his military acts judicial ones, or *vice versa*.   In
his military capacity, therefore, the President is the
mere servant or agent of the civil or political Government, and bound by its action as entirely as would be
General Grant, or any other person, if he had been
appointed such commander-in-chief.   He has no right,
as such commander, to declare war or make peace,
nor decide any question affecting the political relations between the States and the General Government.
If the Congress declare war, whether civil or foreign,
he is, as commander-in-chief, bound by its behests to
use the military and naval forces of the nation for
the subduing of the enemy, and has no further authority than to command them for that purpose.   And
as he has no power, as such commander, to declare war,
so neither, as such, has he power to declare the
war ended, however entire may be the subjugation of
the enemy in his opinion, if the civil Government
shall determine otherwise and direct its further pros-
ecution.   Still less has he any power, as such commander, to dictate or agree upon terms of peace, or to
exonerate the conquered from submission to any such
terms as the civil Government may see fit to impose.
This principle was signally asserted and acted upon
in the surrender by General Johnston of his forces to
General Sherman, and no one ever questioned the
soundness of that decision.   And, if possible, it is still

more clear and certain that he has no power, as such commander, to decide upon or adjust any political relations created by the rebellion between the rebels and the General Government, or to define or determine what may be the legal and political consequences of their treason.

Nor is the power of the President, as the executive head of the nation, less strictly a limited power. With regard to foreign relations, he can make treaties, appoint ambassadors or other ministers and consuls, only by and with the advice and consent of the Senate. His only individual authority, indeed, in regard to such relations, seems to be the unavoidable one of receiving ambassadors and other public ministers. His powers are, in truth, far less than those with which the executive departments under other forms of government are usually invested. They ordinarily have those of declaring war and making peace; whereas, by the Constitution, Congress alone is authorized to declare war, and a treaty of peace can only be concluded by the President with the advice and consent of the Senate. As the executive head of the nation, he, of course, primarily represents the Government in its relations to the Governments of foreign nations, and in all negotiations with them, and may thus exercise a vast influence upon its prosperity and destiny. But he has no power of decision upon the great questions of international obligation, and peace and war, upon which they may chiefly depend.

So, in the administration of the internal affairs of the country, his powers are confined to the appointment of certain judicial and other officers by and with the consent of the Senate, and to taking " care that the laws be faithfully executed." He can neither make laws nor decide finally upon any question arising under those duly enacted. In political questions involving the legal relations of citizens or of the States to the Government, he is subject to the civil Government, which alone has power to decide them. And in judicial questions he is subject to the judiciary.

No principle of public law is more undeniable or more universally recognized, than that the decision of all the possible legal relations of the citizen to the Government, individually or politically, are primarily within the sole and exclusive jurisdiction and rule of the political or legislative department of it; and are never, under any circumstances, within the scope of the executive or of the military power, excepting when invoked for enforcement of the laws concerning them. And nothing can be clearer than that any questions concerning the relations created by the Constitution between the people of the several States, or the States in their corporate capacities, and the Government of the United States; or between the individual States and the other States in the Union, as those relations existed before the rebellion; and concerning any changes or effects upon such relations, caused by

the rebellion ; and concerning the right and power
of the Government to exact indemnity of the rebel
States, and to impose terms or conditions of restoration to their former political powers and privileges,
— are purely questions of constitutional law, of which
the political or legislative department of the Government has primarily exclusive jurisdiction. And no
more flagrantly unconstitutional usurpation of authority can be conceived of, than for the President, as
the executive head of the Government, or as the
commander-in-chief of the army and navy, to assume
the right of deciding upon them as pertaining to him
in either of those capacities. Cases doubtless may
arise, in which it may be impossible seasonably to
determine to which branch of the Government a question demanding immediate decision may belong;
and, in such case, an executive officer may be justifiable in deciding it upon his own responsibility. But
where no reasonable doubt can exist, that it is one,
the decision of which pertains exclusively to the political department of the Government, he can have no
justification in acting upon it in opposition to the
decision of that department, however clear may be
his conviction that such decision is erroneous and
unwarranted by a true construction of the Constitution. The responsibility rests wholly upon that
department, and in no degree upon him. He might
with equal propriety exert his executive or military
power to reverse a judgment of the Supreme Court,

and substitute his sense of justice in place of it, as thus to infringe upon and oppose the jurisdiction of the General Government.

Again, during and upon the termination of the rebellion, the people of the rebel States, as has been shown, and as is conceded in this letter, were utterly disorganized, and without governments which could entitle them to political rights as States in the Union; and could only be re-organized as such States by the consent of the Government of the United States, on its determination that the proper time for such re-organization had come, and of which the Government is confessedly the sole judge.

But it is obvious, that, in deciding upon the right of such restoration and the reception of the representatives of such State into the councils of the nation, the essential preliminary question must be decided, whether the Government thus organized is a republican form of government, and otherwise in harmony with the requisitions of the Constitution. And it is equally clear, that any such question is not only, in its nature, purely political, but that the decision of it is, by the express terms of the Constitution, delegated exclusively to Congress. Upon what principle, then, can it be contended that the President alone, as the executive head of the Government or as commander-in-chief of its forces, is authorized definitely to settle that question, and to recognize the rebel States as entitled to all their political rights and privileges, as, upon this theory in question, he is entitled to do? Can a more palpable substitution of military or executive authority, in place of the political authority established by the Constitution, be conceived of? It is said, indeed, that —

"The mere organization of a republican Government in harmony with the Union of a people of one of the existing States of the United States requires no enabling act, and that no authority is found in the Constitution for any interference by Congress to prohibit or regulate the organization of such a government by the people of an existing State in the Union."

But all this, if true, would not meet the difficulty. Although no previous enabling act may be required to authorize such organization, the subsequent duty and necessity of passing judgment upon the question whether it be a republican form of government, and otherwise in harmony with the Constitution, will nevertheless inevitably arise; and that duty must, as above shown, devolve upon Congress alone. But the proposition is believed to be fallacious, in assuming that the people of a State, which has thus destroyed its political relations to the Union, can, before its re-admission to the Union by the authority of the Government, be accounted with any propriety as " one of the existing States of the United States," or " an existing State in the Union," under the Constitution.

Another and fatal objection, as is believed, to this theory, is found in the consideration that it is based entirely upon the assumption that the recent civil war is to be accounted merely as an insurrection or rebellion, which the executive head of the Government was competent to deal with in determining its nature and extent and its termination. Now, to confound a civil war of the gigantic proportions of that from which the United States is emerging, in which the people of eleven States inhabiting and holding in hostile array about one-half of the territory of the United States, organized themselves into a distinct and separate Government, claiming to be an independent sovereignty, and endeavored by a war of four years in duration, by land and by sea, to establish themselves as an independent nationality, — and to which *de facto* government belligerent rights were accorded by foreign nations and the Government of the United States, and were recognized by all its courts of justice and in its foreign diplomacy, — to confound such a war with a mere insurrection for a redress of grievances, or other causes, against a government whose general authority was acknowledged, and whose nationality it was not its purpose to destroy, and which involved the necessity of nothing more than the exercise of ordinary executive authority to subdue, — seems, to say the least, strangely unreasonable, and to furnish no foundation for any sound conclusions.

The war was in fact, in every sense, a territorial war between two powerful governments, contending, one for national life and the other for the establishment of an empire; calling forth all the resources of the national Government which the most exigent foreign war could put in requisition ; involving it in all the external political relations with other nations which any war could create ; and shaking to their deepest foundations all the internal political relations of the people, and of the loyal and of the rebel States to the Government and the Union. A war in which the executive head of the Government, in the mere exercise of executive authority, would have been utterly powerless and helpless. A war not contemplated nor provided for by the Constitution, perilling the life of the nation, and throwing it back, in self-defence, upon the original principles of self-preservation.

It was a war formally declared by the Confederate Government with all the solemnities of a declaration by a foreign nation, and was finally recognized by an act of Congress, in a statute held by the Supreme Court to be equivalent to a formal declaration of war by that of the United States ; and until which act, a respectable minority of the judges of the Supreme Court held that the President was not justifiable in the exercise of belligerent rights affecting foreign nations. It had therefore every possible element of a foreign war, recognized by the political and judiciary departments of the Government, all whose powers were invoked in its support.

To maintain that the executive head of the Government, by virtue of his office, has sole authority to determine upon the termination of such a war, and

finally to decide upon its consequences upon the
political relations of the parties to it, and the terms of
peace, all which is necessarily involved in this theory,
— and equally so whether he undertakes to dictate
terms of peace, or to decide that none can be constitu-
tionally demanded — seems to vest in the President a
stretch of executive authority utterly abhorrent from
any rational construction of the Constitution, or any
conceivable theory of representative government.

A state of war can only be terminated by a treaty of
peace, express or implied. Usually between foreign
nations, formal written stipulations are executed, and
determine the time and conditions of its cessation.
Where unconditional submission has been exacted,
the rights of war continue on the part of the victor,
until he has pronounced upon the future political con-.
dition of the conquered ; and that, if unresisted, consti-
tutes the final treaty of peace. So here the war,
declared by Congress, — which alone has the power to
declare war, — can only cease when the terms of peace
shall have been finally resolved upon ; and, until then,
the rebels are under the military authority of the Government, excepting in so far as it may see fit to relieve
them from the immediate exercise of such authority,
during its pleasure. But peace will not have terminated
the war, until it shall have been decided on what terms
the rebel States shall be restored to the Union, or that
no terms can or shall be exacted. And that decision
cannot rest with the Executive. In the case of a

foreign war, it would be the duty of the Senate, acting in concert with the Executive, to determine on what terms the war should cease, or, in other words, when and how peace should be made. But in a civil war like this, where the fundamental relations of the people of the rebel States to the Constitution and the laws are involved, it is plain that the only departments which have cognizance of them, or can decide them, are the political or judiciary departments. The idea that the commander-in-chief of the forces of a Government, acting merely as such, can decide the question when a war declared by the authority of Congress has ended, and its purposes have been accomplished, is too absurd to require refutation. He is the mere servant or instrument of the Government in carrying on the war ; and must prosecute it, and continue the exercise of military authority against and over the enemy, whatever may be his individual opinion, until the Goverment decide the war to be ended by agreeing upon terms of peace. Nor, upon examination, is the idea that the Executive Department of the Government can decide such a question in the case of a war like this any more tenable, it having been shown that such decision necessarily involves the determination of many other questions purely political and constitutional, of which the Executive Department has no jurisdiction.

In conclusion, whatever questions might be raised concerning the powers of Congress, or of the Executive in ordinary cases of insurrection, it is believed

that in the case of a war declared by Congress, which
alone has the power to declare war, and which power
is not limited by the Constitution to a foreign, but
applies, with equal reason, to a civil war of a magni-
tude to require its interposition, — and in view of the
unusual restraints imposed by the Constitution of the
United States upon the Executive in relation to all
matters of peace and war, — it is believed that no reasonable doubt can exist, that the President has no
authority whatever to decide upon the terms or conditions of peace, or upon those of the restoration of the
belligerents subdued by force of arms to their former
political rights and privileges in the Union.

Many other arguments might be adduced in support
of the authority claimed by Congress, and there are
doubtless others in defence of the President's policy
which have not been particularly noticed in the preceding remarks.

It is believed, however, that the main points on
both sides have been considered as fully as the nature
of a publication of this sort will permit, and that they
embrace in substance the merits of the question before
the country.   The author is conscious that there is a
limit to the patience of readers, and beyond which he
has great apprehension that he has already trans-
gressed.

He cannot, however, leave the subject without
adverting to a possible misapprehension of his views
upon the importance and sacredness of the rights of

the States under the Constitution, which might arise
from the nature of the discussion which has been
attempted. It will be observed, that his only object
has been to vindicate the sovereignty of the General
Government against the assaults made upon it by
advocates of the rights of inhabitants of States who
had renounced allegiance to it, and had engaged in
civil war for its overthrow; and consequently, that
the discussion has been almost exclusively confined to consideration of the relations of the States
to the General Government in that aspect only, and
of the subordination and limitations of State sovereignty rather than of its attributes. But no one
can be more profoundly impressed, than he believes
himself to be, with the essential importance and in-
violability of the rights intended to be secured to the
several States under the Constitution. He accounts
their individual sovereignty and independence over the
domestic relations and municipal law, and in the
internal governments of their respective inhabitants,
as the very foundation stones of the national Government. The preservation of this sovereignty and
independence, to the fullest extent warranted by the
Constitution, he considers to be chief among the fun
damental principles of American statesmanship; as the
only means possible of maintaining a free and ener-
getic government over territories of extent so vast as
those already comprised within our national bounda-
ries; as the safest barrier against attempt at Executive

usurpation ; as the main bulwark against the natural
tendency of the General Government, as of all others, to consolidation and centralization of its authority ; and which, not thus controlled, attaining at first to
the exercise of arbitrary power by the many, would,
as all history prophesies, eventually terminate in
practical despotism ; and, above all, as the sufficient
and only instrumentality for educating and disciplining
successive generations in the knowledge and practice
of political rights and duties, by which alone they
can be made capable of self-government.

And no one will hail with profounder gladness a
just perception on the part of the inhabitants of the
rebel States of their true relations to the Government, and their return to their constitutional places
in the Union which, unhappily for us all, they have
made vacant.

www.ingramcontent.com/pod-product-compliance
Lightning Source LLC
Chambersburg PA
CBHW030612270326
41927CB00007B/1139